# Parental Guidance

## Long Distance Care for Aging Parents

Ana McGinley

Get the latest updates:
www.parentalguidance.info

Join the community:
https://www.facebook.com/parentalguidancebook

Contact Ana:
hello@parentalguidance.info

# TABLE OF CONTENTS

Introduction .......... i

Your Parent Faces A Health Crisis and Needs Help ... 1

How Can You Help? .......... 17

Families .......... 31

Communication .......... 49

Common Chronic Diseases Of The Elderly .......... 59

Safety Within the Home .......... 73

Risks Outside The Home .......... 95

Legal and Financial Matters .......... 107

Overview of Care For An Aging Parent .......... 121

Closing Thoughts .......... 127

Acknowledgements .......... 131

Bibliography .......... 133

# INTRODUCTION

> The great secret that all old people share is that you really haven't changed in seventy or eighty years. Your body changes, but you don't change at all. And that, of course, causes great confusion.
>
> Doris Lessing

Even though I am solidly middle-aged, this quote from Doris Lessing rings true for me. While the outside world may notice my eyes have been lined by the stress of raising teenagers, my body is marked by operational and accidental scars, and my bust-line is being enticed to meet up with my waistline - I vehemently insist that I am still the same person I have always been. The same young woman depicted enjoying herself in photos taken two decades ago. Admittedly I'm considerably more cynical, more responsible, and less tolerant of dim-witted behavior – but these attributes came with entry into adulthood and its subgroup, parenthood.

Age does not change the person you are. It may change the life you lead, but it does not alter the inner being that is you. The same is true for all people, including our parents. Take as an example my 80-year-old mother-in-law. Always a world explorer who continues to want to be actively involved in things that matter, she still embarks on excursions to the different parts of the planet that spark her interest. Her current plans are to visit far North Canada (for the Northern lights), Australia's Northern Territory (a joint visit with her older sister to a place that neither has visited previously), and to come to the Netherlands (to visit with us). Most outsiders would not credit this octogenarian with the spunk to follow her itchy feet – especially as she has chronic problems with pain in her back and hips, something she tries not to mention. With a lack of acute health problems, she too remains the same as her 20-year-old self, although I suspect her taste for fine whisky came later in life.

Age does not need to be the wet blanket that stops people living the lives they love. But here is the rub. With increasing age comes increased risk of suffering acute and chronic health problems. It is these attacks on healthy bodies that jeopardize the individual's capacity to be independent.

About forty years ago I came to the sad realization that my father was not going to live forever. This rude awakening came to me on the evening of my father's 40th birthday. When my father came to investigate the reason for my distress, I cried and told him that he only had sixty years left to live. I remember being annoyed at having to explain to him that 40 plus 60 equals 100 – which was the point of death, and that his birthday marked yet another year closer to his imminent demise. As a six-year-old child I was better with numbers than biology.

My father is now 76. In the last five years, he has faced some debilitating health problems: a heart attack, mini-strokes (TIAs), diabetes, arthritis, loss of teeth, and memory problems. The sum tally of his health complaints has rendered him into a very thin man in constant pain needing 15 hours of sleep per day, who can't walk further than 50 metres and avoids social occasions. He finds the idea of being alive to celebrate his 100th birthday depressing.

I live in the Netherlands, approximately 15,000kms from my parents who are based in an Australian rural town, once famous for its abattoirs and the prime beef that came out of their doors. Although they have lived in this town for four decades they have become increasingly socially isolated, as their close friends relocate to the capital city to be closer to their own adult children.

My three siblings live within a 3km radius of my parent's home and have varying degrees of regular contact with them, and each other. Just like my parents, it has been decades since they have had close relationships with one another. Not interesting enough for reality television, we are your average, moderately dysfunctional family.

I last saw my parents about two years ago. The flight home takes a minimum of 30 hours, reducing the available time I have to be away from my own family of six, and in Australia with my parents. Twice I have made this trip following serious health scares with my father. On both occasions I was home again within 12 days, physically and mentally exhausted, and frustrated with the lack of personal involvement I could offer to ensure that my father received the health care services necessary to improve his quality of life.

An integral disclosure central to my reasons for wanting to write this book is that I have 15 years of professional experience as a specialist aged care social worker. I have worked in hospitals, community health centres, aged care assessment teams, memory disorder clinics, older adult mental health services, residential care facilities, legal tribunals and for the Alzheimer Association. My work has given me many opportunities to advocate and support older adults at times when they need help due to illness and age-related disabilities.

This book is the combination of professional knowledge and personal experiences – my own and those of the friends and acquaintances who have confronted similar challenges in remaining involved with parents who live in different towns, states and countries, as they face health problems that impact on their independence. It is a guide to maintaining relationships so aging parents feel our love and support at times when they feel vulnerable and alone. In addition this book offers essential information to enable you to be an active and useful participant in their health care plan – even though you may be thousands of kilometres away.

Ana McGinley

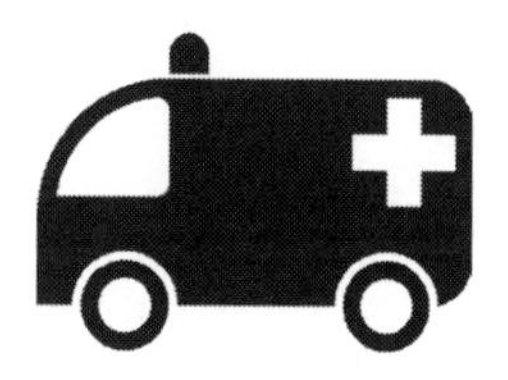

# Your Parent Faces A Health Crisis and Needs Help

- The dreaded phone call (a case scenario)
- To stay or go
- Essential information needed to make a decision
- Practical considerations
- Days later
- Weeks later
- Bumps on the road
- A month later
- When offering help is met with resistance
- Life's spunk
- Our own need to help

## The Dreaded Phone Call

Imagine yourself in this scenario:

It is the early hours of the morning. You are abruptly awoken by the sound of a telephone demanding to be answered. The caller tells you that your mother has been taken to hospital and is in the intensive care unit. The information available is limited, although you elicit that your mother has had a stroke and that, at this stage, it is too early to tell what damage the stroke has caused. You thank the caller, hang up, and enter into that transient state of shock that accompanies bad news.

Your mother lives alone in Brisbane, Australia. Three years ago your husband was offered a great job opportunity in Singapore, resulting in the gleeful packing up of the family and a move to Asia. You phone your sister, who lives in Sydney (1000kms from Brisbane) and is busy working as an architect while raising a young family. She is distraught and convinced that your mother may die at any moment. She has made plans to be in Brisbane by the early evening. She tells you that you must come.

## To Stay Or Go?

Honestly, there is no right answer.

Everyone will have an opinion, including the sometimes uttered: "You will never forgive yourself if you don't get to say goodbye". The truth is, there is no correct answer and no wrong answer. This is a decision you need to make for yourself. So, take a breath.

Making your *right decision* will involve listening to your heart, your head, and your stomach. Many factors will influence the decision you make including the severity of the health problem; the relationship you have with your parent; your ability to drop your current role for a period of time and the availability of someone else to take on your responsibilities; finances; available flights; and likely prognosis (recovery, or a risk that the person will die before you arrive).

Some people will leave immediately, others will wait until a clear prognosis is available, and some family members will decide not to go at all. Whatever your decision is, acknowledge that the sudden illness of a family member is a time of great anxiety.

## Essential Information Needed To Make A Decision:

Before you determine whether or not to pack you bag, you will need to elicit answers to the questions that will impact on your plans. As it is a stressful time, it may be wise to enlist the support of a clear-thinking family member or friend to help ensure you have all the answers you need to make your decision.

First question – *what is the name of the hospital?* If your parent lives in a large city, there may be many hospitals, so getting the correct name and address of the hospital will be the first crucial piece of information you need. In the case of a parent admitted to the only hospital in a small town, it is useful to know whether the hospital has the technology and specialist staff to provide the best care options. If not, what are the chances that your parent will be transferred to a larger, better-equipped hospital in a larger city. My father (and mother) have been flown to the capital city on two occasions for scans and specialist appointments not available in either of the two hospitals that service the town they live in. Knowing that a transfer to another hospital is required will impact on any flight plans you may make.

*Who is the best staff person to contact for up-to-date information about your parent?*

In my own professional experience, most medical specialists working in hospitals will hand down the task of talking on the phone to family members to their registrar and interns. Get all the names so that you have a list of medical staff to approach for information. Find out the best time to phone and if possible email any questions you may have before you phone, so that answers are ready.

Often it is more productive to find out the names of the Nurse Unit Manager and Social Worker assigned to the unit. The Nurse Unit Manager (also known as the Charge Nurse, Matron, Senior Nurse) will be able to alert you to any changes faster than medical staff. When the Nurse Unit Manager is not physically available, another nurse will be holding the position. Nurses have access to all medical files, attend daily meetings with doctors and allied health staff, and see the patients frequently during each shift.

Social workers are often considered the conduit between the hospital staff, family and community services. Although social workers have a bad rap as being the "touchy feely" health professionals, their influence ensures that patients are seen as "whole people" rather than as medical issues. Their expertise lies in assessing the individual and their family support system, and then coordinating available services to ensure that, on leaving the hospital, identified individual needs are adequately met.

*The collection of information is a two-way street.*

Ask the questions you feel you need to ask. Provide answers to the questions you are asked by the treating team, even if the questions seem irrelevant or random to you. These questions are asked for a specific purpose. When you don't know the answer or information that is being asked – if is okay to admit that you don't know. Good intentions and the retelling of a funny old family story will not assist in making a timely diagnosis.

*Do your own research, starting with achieving a basic understanding of the diagnosis.*

For example: was the stroke an ischemic stroke or a hemorrhagic stroke? What is the prognosis and recommended treatment?

So you are now at the point where you have all essential information about your mother or father's current medical condition and treatment plan. Especially in the case of a stroke, this may change quickly during the first few days. Making your decision to go to your parent is still pending. Following are additional issues that may further influence your decision to stay or go.

## Practical Considerations

*If you decide to go, these practical questions will need answers:*

- How will you get to your parent – plane, train, bus or car? For many people the fastest option will be by plane, hence the following questions refer to plane travel. Substitute train or bus as needed.
- When is the next available flight? Is there a seat available? Is this a direct flight or a flight with multiple stops. Often it is faster to wait a day for a direct flight then to have the frustration of being stuck in an airport waiting hours for a connecting flight. Do you have the finances to pay for the ticket – if not, where can you access the money needed?
- If you plan to drive, is it possible to use your own car – or will you need to rent a car?

- If you are responsible for the care of children, sick adults or pets – is someone able to take on these responsibilities while you are away?
- If you are working, are you able to leave your work to be with sick relatives? Is there a limit to the time you are able to be away from your job?
- What commitments do you have in the next month? Can you cancel or delay these commitments?
- Where will you stay? Can you stay in your parent's home? Do you have a key to get in? Do you have friends or other family members you can stay with? If not, know what your accommodation budget is before contacting a travel agent or searching the Internet looking for accommodation options.

## Days Later

You made a decision and are now either spending a lot of time at the hospital or at home, worried about your mother and what the future will hold for her. Her condition has improved and she is being transferred from intensive care to the stroke care unit for more assessments and monitoring. Early tests indicate that the ischemic stroke she sustained has resulted in weakness on the left side of her body, obvious when she walks or uses her left arm and hand. Her speech and vision have also been affected by the stroke, yet luckily the residual damage from the stroke has not left her immobile and dependent. She has been given medications and been referred to the rehabilitation team to improve the strength on her left side.

## Weeks Later

Your mother is due to be discharged at the end of the week. In the last two weeks your sister has returned to Sydney. You have spoken to doctors, physiotherapists, occupational therapists, discharge nurses and social workers. The plan is for your mother to be discharged home from the hospital.

Following an assessment by the Occupational Therapist, some minor modifications have been made to your mother's home (rails in the toilet and bathroom, rugs removed, fire alarms installed). Your mother has agreed to a three-month program of physical rehabilitation based at the hospital. You purchased a personal alarm pendant that your mother promises she will wear at all times.

The doctors have told your mother that she cannot drive until further notice. The social worker has arranged a weekly shopping service, house-cleaning service, transport to the hospital, and a weekly visit from a volunteer – knowing that your mother lives alone and will be unable to initiate visits to her friends who do not live in the same suburb.

All these arrangements (which can be done in person or from afar) seem to be in place and the system is working well. Your mother goes home, and your life returns to normal.

## Bumps On The Road

After her discharge from hospital, you phone your mother every few days. She tells you that she feels fine and is happy to be home again. The bi-weekly physiotherapy sessions make her tired, but the strength in her left side is slowly returning. She complains about not being able to drive her car and having to rely on the community shopping service to bring the things she wants. Although receiving regular phone calls from friends, visitors are limited to the occasional neighbour, the volunteer visitor and the social worker.

Consider how your mother's life has changed in the past month. Previously she called all the shots. She shopped, visited friends, gardened, went to the theatre and the cinema, planned holidays, went to church, and kept in contact with distant friends and family via email.

The stroke has taken away her independence and made her feel anxious and vulnerable. She is frustrated that her life decisions have been taken over by a group of strangers from the hospital and community health services. The hospital sends the patient transport van to collect her for the rehabilitation program. The van parks out the front of her house, exposing her private life to her neighbours. The shopping service volunteer has plenty of ideas about what should be on her shopping list. The volunteer visitor drives her nuts with inane conversation.

The complaints slip out. You tell her that it is only for a short time, she needs the help, and that she agreed to the plan. It is frustrating for you both.

## A Month Later

Your mother stops complaining to you two weeks before the social worker phones to tell you that your mother is refusing the home help services. She no longer wants strangers in her home. She plans to ask the neighbour for help buying groceries. Being a feisty and independent woman, this decision fits her personality. As she is mentally competent she has the right to refuse services, especially as she is billed, albeit a minimal amount, for the community services she receives. This doesn't lessen the concerns that both you and your sister have for your mother and your belief that someone should be there to help and check on her safety.

## When Offering Help Is Met With Resistance

Last week I spoke with my own father in Australia. He told me that he is sick of my sister always telling him what to do. He said that she is always hassling him to see different doctors and to have new tests done and complained that she was coming over to take him to have a specialist appointment about his feet. I called my sister who said that she had taken both my parents to the three appointments they had agreed to in discussions with his general physician. These appointments were to check whether he had tumours; a follow-up appointment with the heart specialist; and for more investigations of his back pain. Today they were due to see someone about his memory problems.

Just like toddlers are considered to be contrary, demanding and obstinate, old people are often depicted as being cantankerous, crotchety and stubborn. Interesting similarities in behavioral traits based on individuals, young and old, striving to hold on to their independence. While toddlers are finding their independence, older people are often faced with the threat of losing theirs. This threat is enough to make anyone grumpy and resistant even if, like my father, you aren't really sure what is going on. (Penn State, 2015)

Arranging assistance and helping an older person who needs, but doesn't want, help – is enough to exasperate most family members. Yet accepting that resistance is futile is often indicative of someone who has thrown down the towel and is giving up the fight that has made them who they are.

## Life's Spunk

About ten years ago I was referred a gentleman who had been diagnosed with dementia and was exhibiting some "challenging behaviors". The man had a tendency to jam his wife's oxygen tubing under chair legs or in doorways, blocking the oxygen she needed due to her emphysema. The wife was afraid that he was trying to kill her and agreed to his admission to a secure unit at the hospital for assessment.

Every shift, I spent time with him hoping for a lucid moment allowing me to uncover a little more of his personal story. Eventually our timing coincided and he launched into a tale padded with old memories, but lacking insight about his current predicament.

He said that as a young man he had owned a hotel in a rural Australian town. His memories of training the local rugby team, a culturally mixed team drawing members from local farms and aboriginal communities, gave him obvious joy. He described his relationship with his wife as always being fiery, explaining that they were both strong-willed individuals. Later, both his wife and daughter confirmed his story, including his description of their relationship.

Unfortunately, he could not recall or offer any reason why he would try to block his wife's oxygen supply. The treating team were left to surmise that without any obvious will to harm his wife, the underlying reasons for this behavior were based on his frustration at feeling he was being held captive inside their apartment while his wife told him what to do.

This was the point that their lives had reached: the wife was restricted to a wheelchair and 24 hour oxygen therapy, and the husband was not considered safe to leave the apartment alone due to his dementia.

We will never know for certain why this man fiddled with the oxygen tubing. As he exhibited no obvious inclinations to harm his wife and was deemed mentally incompetent due to his dementia, probable cause for his actions was focused on subconscious psychological (personality, relationship issues, need for independence) and environmental factors. Sadly, he ended up being discharged to a dementia specific residential care facility where his freedom was even more compromised.

The moral of the tale is that even when they are sick, our parents remain individuals shaped by their own history and driven by their unique personality. This is especially so if they suffer from a dementia.

## Our Own Need to Help

Most of us have an inherent need to make things right for our parents should they become sick or frail. We don't want to see them deprived of the help and health care they need. Sometimes we want this more than they want it themselves.

As adult children living away from our aging parents we are limited in the amount of hands-on help we can provide. To compensate, we can ensure that the opportunity for our parent to receive assistance is available by liaising with the health care team and providing all essential information about our parent and their wishes. By doing so, the chance of the discharge plan being accepted by parents is increased. We can support them as they become aware of the consequences of ending up in hospital, and how this is going to have long-lasting effects on their lifestyle and independence. Mostly we can remind them that they are invaluable members of our lives, when everyone else around them will see them as a reduced version of themselves.

> "Old Age is not a disease - it is a strength and survivorship, triumph over all kinds of vicissitudes and disappointments, trials and illnesses"
>
> Maggie Kuhn

# How Can You Help?

- Reducing the distance factor
- Communication is not for dummies
- Let's meet the players (Identifying health care staff)
- Do your own research
- Being realistic with plans
- Keeping the main player (your parent) in the spotlight
- Checklist for long distance caregivers

Don't let the last section of Chapter One make you despondent. Understanding the psychology behind why accepting help may be difficult for an older person is essential for all family and professional care providers. Comprehending this response is useful in introducing a care plan that your parent will agree with and adhere to in the months or years that extra help is required. And really, that is the point.

## Reducing The Distance Factor

Distance should not stop you being able to participate in conversations about future plans for your parent. As a close family member you have a right, some people would argue responsibility, to be part of this process. This is especially true when you are an only child, or if your parent is cognitively unable to make their own decisions. You have a long history of knowing your parent – their likes, dislikes and habits – so are well-equipped to be their advocate and ensure that plans are made to their benefit.

*Being involved from a distance is about:*

- communication;
- researching possibilities;
- knowing practicalities;
- keeping an open discussion with your parent to ensure that they know and agree with what is going on around them.

## Communication Is Not for Dummies

First step communication is aimed at collecting information and usually takes place via telephone. It is recommended that you have a list of the names of people who are involved in looking after your parent – and both email and phone contact details. This was briefly covered earlier, yet is worth repeating, as obtaining the information you need the first, and not the fifth, time you make contact will save you time and frustration.

Secondly, make a list of what information you are seeking when you speak to hospital or community health care staff. This will make it easier to identify whom you should be aiming to make contact with. For example, if you want to know the results of a MRI test, you need to speak to medical staff. To discuss the implementation of home based care services, you will most likely need to speak with the social worker.

A benefit to writing down a list of questions is that your focus is on the practical aspects of the situation that need attention. Health care staff can only provide limited emotional support to family members, especially when they are not physically present. Try not to waste your phone call with emotion, instead milk it for the information you need. If you have many questions, it is good to pre-book a time to make a phone or Skype call, so staff can be better prepared. Alternatively, sending an email with your questions prior to making phone contact may help ensure correct information is given to you.

The following section has been included for people who are unfamiliar with the people and professionals that may be involved in the care of their parent, both in the hospital and community health care sector.

## Let's Meet the Players

I have never met any saints working in hospitals, yet the majority of health care staff chose their profession because they care about people. Staff are often over worked in an underfunded working environment. This does not mean that your parent will receive substandard care, but it does mean that you may experience, on occasion, a lack of adequate time to converse with staff, especially in acute care units.

Located at the top of the hospital and health care hierarchy are Medical Specialists – including geriatricians, psychogeriatricians, cardiac specialists, oncologists, renal specialists, orthopaedic surgeons, neurologists, etc. Medical specialists are doctors who focus on a specific body part or body system. Each specialist will have his or her own batch of tests that will indicate whether the health problem they have been asked to consult on is part of their service.

Older people rarely have their medical treatment limited to the sole care of one specialist during a hospital admission. This is because as bodies age, they start to deteriorate and the chance of multiple chronic health problems increases. In the past year my father has seen a heart specialist, arthritis specialist, eye specialist, general physician (there are no psychogeriatricians available to check memory problems), chiropodist, hospital dentist, diabetes specialist and a neurologist. He has a busier calendar of appointments than I do.

For people over the age of 70 with multiple health problems, it is wise to have their medical care managed by one specialist, preferably a geriatrician. A geriatrician is skilled in understanding the impact of disease on older bodies. They are also knowledgeable about the effect medications have on older people, especially when they are taking numerous medications for different problems. Most geriatricians also have the people skills needed to understand the issues of older people, and a little more patience to hear their stories.

When a geriatrician is not available, request that your parent be placed under the care of a general physician. If your parent has been diagnosed with a dementia or mental illness, request a referral to a psychogeriatrician.

In all medical systems there is a hierarchy of doctors who have different titles dependent on their years of training. Basically, decisions are made by doctors who sit at the top of the hierarchy – with much of the actual work being allocated down the line. Below is a basic explanation of the medical hierarchy in Australia. Although job titles may differ in other countries, the hierarchy will remain similar.

Medical interns have graduated with medical degrees and are in the first year of their hospital (supervised) program that will see them rotate through different medical units. Next comes a Junior House Officer (JHO), Senior House Officer (SHO), Principal House Officer (PHO) with respectively one, two and three years of hospital-based experience under their belts. Registrars have completed three years of hospital-based experience and have been subsequently accepted into a training program for a specific clinical specialty like geriatrics or oncology. The medical specialists in hospitals are Senior Medical Officers (SMO) holding senior positions in a hierarchy of doctors who are in training to reach this top level of their careers.

As with medical staff, Nursing staff also have their own management structure based on education, experience and training. Each unit in a hospital will have an allocated Nurse Unit Manager (Charge Nurse, Matron), with senior nurses, junior nurses – and nurse specialists who consult on best practice measures for specific nursing care issues like wound management or incontinence.

The Social Worker plays a major role in working with family members. This includes compiling a biopsychosocial assessment on the person admitted to hospital. Deciphering the jargon, this basically means that the social worker will ask many questions to discover who the person was before they were admitted to the hospital. Questions will cover all major markers in your parent's life – birthplace, any significant incidents during childhood, education, work history, marriage and family, daily routines, stressors, and any problems they encountered in living independently.

The social worker identifies the availability of support from family, friends or other people involved in your parent's life. They will ask about finances and future financial plans (e.g. power of attorney, advanced care directives, wills).

Physiotherapists help people improve their range of movement via manual therapy, exercise and education. For older clients physiotherapists are important major players following a stroke, orthopaedic surgery (knee or hip replacements), people with Parkinson's disease, and for people limited by arthritis.

Occupational therapists are skilled in restoring functional abilities needed for independence. They assess the person and the environment making recommendations for changes that will improve independence and safety. A good example is installing rails in the shower and toilet so that people with mobility and balance problems are able to support themselves.

Speech therapists work with people who have speech and swallowing problems. Speech therapy is often required in the rehabilitation of people who have suffered a stroke.

Psychologists assess and treat cognitive problems, mood disorders, coping mechanisms, emotional disturbances and behavioral problems. Psychologists evaluate the referred problem and, when indicated, offer a time limited treatment program. Psychologists are often referred older people with depression or anxiety problems.

Community Health Care Services provide staff to visit an older person in their home. Most of these services provide nursing care, domestic assistance, transport or social support. Depending on the reason for the visit, the staff can be trained nurses, accredited care staff, untrained staff, or volunteers.

## Do Your Own Research

Equip yourself by finding out everything you can about your parent's condition and the difficulties it causes in their life. Research prognosis, treatment options, medications, associated problems with mobility/cognition/functioning. Educate yourself about what is happening to your parent now and what will most likely happen in the future. Knowledge will keep you grounded.

Investigate what services are available to help your parent if they are discharged home from the hospital. Who will arrange the services? What, if any, forms do you need to complete for admission to the service? What are the costs involved? Are customer reviews of these services available?

If the discharge plan involves a move to a residential care facility, your choices may seem limited to the facilities where there are vacancies at the time the medical team decides your parent needs to be discharged from the hospital. There is always pressure to move patients who are not receiving active medical treatment, yet discharging to a facility not agreed to by the person and their family is not acceptable.

Be proactive by adding residential care facilities to your research list. Find out what is available, what level of care (high care, low care, aging-in-place, dementia care) is provided and whether the facility will guarantee that your parent can remain in the facility should their care needs increase.

Is respite care available at the facility? Respite is a term generally related to caregivers: it is the time that caregivers get a break from providing care for someone.

Having respite available also means that your parent may be able to spend a few weeks in the facility (when approved by the relevant government accredited aged care team), to check whether they are happy to stay permanently.

## Be Realistic With Plans

This section is about keeping your research real. Knowing what your parent needs, wants and will agree to - and then matching a service that can meet these requirements ensures that everybody wins. Not matching up both sides of this equation can result in short-lived arrangements that need to be reassessed by you. A good example is that of many older people agreeing to referrals for formal help with cleaning their homes, and then cancelling when they discover that there is a cost involved.

*Asking for help needs to be specific to the individual.* Below is an example of a man who lived alone and needed assistance. This man had been referred to community service without either the referring agency or community service intake officer visiting in person to correctly assess what help he required. Family members can ensure that the help being offered is actually the help that their parent needs.

During my years as an expat in Singapore I coordinated volunteers to work in local charity organizations. In this role, I spent a day with a health care service that delivered food to socially isolated elderly people who had been discharged home after a stay in hospital. On this day, we carried six kilos of uncooked rice to a man who lived alone in an apartment on a social housing complex. The man who opened the door had an open gap in his face from his lower lip to where his nose should have been, the result of cancer attacking the palates in his mouth. His small lounge room was piled with bags of uncooked rice. Although he had received this service for some time, nobody had noticed that this man was unable to eat rice or anything else that couldn't go through a straw.

Practical considerations include knowing past likes and habits (especially regarding accepting help from strangers); finances; home ownership – and other options to formal home help services that are available to meet care needs.

## Keeping the Main Player in the Spotlight

Unfortunately, this needs to be said: your parent should be present in meetings discussing their care. They have a right to know what is being said and planned for them. This is also true for people with dementia, even when it appears that they are not able to follow the conversation. Often a legal guardian is appointed with powers to make decisions regarding medical care, home based care services and/or accommodation for people who are cognitively impaired due to dementia, other mental illnesses or brain injuries. The guardian has the legal responsibility to make these decisions on behalf of the person – yet must give serious consideration to any perturbation the person shows in making decisions.

## Checklist For Long Distance Caregivers

- Ensure you have the telephone number and email addresses of hospital staff, and that they are aware that you want to be involved in the care of your parent.
- Find out as much as you can about your parent's health condition. What will their diagnosis

mean for them in the future? Have an idea what kind of help they will need in the coming months and years.

- Get on the Internet and find out everything you can about aged care services and facilities in the area your parent lives. Get a list of options and make contact with the manager of these organizations to discuss the practical aspects that include waiting lists, costs, and range of services available.
- Keep open a running conversation with your parent about what is going on around them. Make sure that their wishes are paramount in discussions with health care staff. Be conscious of a possible need to have a guardian appointed if your parent becomes cognitively impaired.
- Maintain regular contact with other family members. Support through family cohesion will help to ensure the best outcome for your parent.

# FAMILIES

- When illness and the need for help alter the parent-child dynamic
- Sandwich caregivers
- Differing expectations
- What happens when you don't like your parent
- Team plan – appointing a family manager
- Spousal caregivers

"There's nothing that makes you more insane than family. Or more happy. Or more exasperated. Or more... secure."
Jim Butcher

Our relationships with our family members change with time. Childhood is often a time of conflict as children compete for attention from parents. My sister and I hated one another as kids but now in our 40s are able to enjoy spending a week together without bickering or trying to stab one another with scissors. Similarly our relationships with our parents transform as we mature and become independent of them. This does not guarantee that the parent-child relationship improves. Often the parent-child relationship does not improve, yet it matters less because the adult child is no longer dependent on the parent.

## When Illness and the Need For Help Alter the Parent-Child Dynamic

My cousin is an only child. She married late and moved a few Dutch provinces away from her parents. By the time she had given birth to her second child, her parents had packed up the family home and moved into an apartment about 5kms from their daughter. Initially my cousin loved that her parents were close enough to drop by for a coffee, to water the plants when she was on holidays, and to help look after her children. My uncle and aunt are typical of many older Dutch people. Their days are filled with appointments: volunteer work, bridge club, choir practice, bike trips and social engagements. Subsequently it was less than a year before my cousin was complaining that her hopes for some free family child-care had diminished. Worse still, she could envisage her future with aging parents in the neighbourhood. Ten years later her fears have been realized as both parents have celebrated their 81st birthday and battle a variety of health complaints.

If both your parents are alive, their care needs must be assessed individually. This scenario can be complicated. (Further consideration will be given at the end of this section.)

## Sandwich caregivers

The official term for a person (usually a woman) who is caring for both children and a parent (or parents) is a "sandwich" caregiver. In the UK alone, the sandwich generation of caregivers accounts for around 2.4 million people. (Drakakis 2013)

This phenomenon of caregivers continues to rise as women delay having children and pursue their careers longer; housing prices increase; older children remain at home; and health care advances increase longevity. The end result is monstrous strain on families, especially women. The pressure is both financial and practical, often resulting in a woman giving up her career to care for older family members. In comparison to other caregivers, sandwich generation caregivers are at high risk of depression and burnout. (Holzhausen 2014)

The concept of a sandwich generation of caregivers is accepted and expected in some cultures. For example in many Asian cultures, the idea that families exclusively care for their elderly continues to permeate through generations especially in less developed countries without an existing system of subsidized community health care services.

My maternal grandmother was a Maltese matriarch who migrated to Australia with her husband and ten children and set up house in central Sydney. She ran her house and family as if she was still living in Malta.

Her acquisition of English was minimal; she only socialized with other Maltese people; cooked Maltese food; and relied solely on her family as she grew older.

Problems arose when her expectation, that in her later years she would be cared for by her adult daughters, was not met to her satisfaction. She truly believed that one of her daughters should leave her own husband and family to live in my grandmother's house, to clean my grandmother's house to her own unique standards, to cook meals following her methods, and to provide constant companionship as she complained about her many health problems. She refused to accept that her daughters had their own children, jobs and lives – making them unavailable and unwilling to take on this role.

Then I moved to Sydney. My grandmother was keen to have me come and stay with her. Being a poor student, I agreed. It didn't last very long. I was willing to help out, but there was little time to enjoy Sydney and my new friends and to satisfactorily meet her expectations of me - as a female family member - living in her house. She never let up her belief that as the matriarch of a large family she deserved to be cared for in her dotage by her daughters. Apparently this is what she would have done for her own mother, if she hadn't moved continents.

## Differing Expectations

Our parents' expectations of us have always been a source of conflict. Case in point, I am not actually a doctor or a lawyer as my parents had hoped. Similarly, if my own kids meet all my expectations regarding working hard at school; wearing respectable clothing; spouting interesting conversation; being polite; having admirable friends; and resisting all my own bad habits – they will one day be wealthy neurosurgeons too dull to have any fun with.

Conversations with our parents aimed at planning for a time when they may need our help should happen long before this time arrives. This specific discussion may start with wishes, yet needs to end with what is actually possible should illness or disability result in the need for help. Older people have already had the experience of their own parents or relatives aging and needing help. This experience will have formed their own opinions about how they would like to live in their later years.

*Topics that need to be covered are:*

- who is available to help;
- what formal services exist locally;
- accommodation;
- finances (e.g. some government services are means tested), and
- legal considerations (e.g. is there a power of attorney).

At this stage, the aim of the discussion is to identify what is available (both informally and formally) and to make sure that there are no obvious reasons that future help might be refused. Leaving the discussion with a list of acceptable options is a good result. For example, if your parent lives in an isolated town without community care services – would they be willing to advertise and pay someone to help clean the house? Or, would they consider moving to a larger town with available home care services?

Due to pride, privacy or feeling vulnerable, some people will not want to have this conversation with their adult children. My father is one of these people. Although, he has been planning his funeral – in a loud, joking manner – for about 20 years, the family response has always been to ignore him. He pretends that these discussions are funny, even when nobody else is laughing. They seem to conceal his fear of aging and being placed in a nursing home. Strange, as he is the only person who has ever mentioned residential care.

I mention my father as an example of the unspoken fears that often skirt these conversations. Getting older comes with increased awareness of one's vulnerability. At this stage of life it is common to be in contact with siblings, spouses, friends and acquaintances that are sick and suffering. Disease and death are more common than at any other life stage, and hence it remains on the minds of many older people. My father worked in a large residential care facility for older people. Five days a week he was with elderly people who could not live in their own homes for various health reasons.

Previously a social person, he enjoyed meeting new residents and greeting the long stay residents. He rarely entered the high care unit that provided care for people in the end stage of life, yet he attended many funerals. His jokes are based on his own fears, making it difficult for him to fully participate in plans for his own future.

---

Ana McGinley

## What Happens When You Don't Actually Like Your Parents?

Guilt tripping people into caring for others is a recipe for disaster. Caregivers who take on this role filled with resentment place the person they care for at risk, while filling their own lives with unnecessary stress.

There are numerous reasons that this situation may arise including childhood abuse and neglect; unresolved adult conflict; and even personality changes in the aging parent (common in people with dementia). If this is the case, look for alternatives that will result in necessary care being provided by someone other than you. This is your life, your call.

A friend's mother has early-moderate level dementia and continues to live in her own home. My friend hates to visit her because her mother spends the entire visit complaining about life, the family and about her. As a mother of two young children, my friend reported that after visiting her mother, she is left feeling irritated and depressed. Her husband and children then suffer her low moods and short temper until the visit works itself out of her system.

Being proactive, she came up with a simple and effective solution. My friend has exchanged 'mother visiting duties' with a girlfriend who also has a mother with dementia. This means that each week my friend visits her friend's mother – and vice versa.

My friend limits her visits to her own mother to times that she feels strong enough to cope with her mother's negativity. Her plan ensures her mother has a weekly visitor and that she remains up-to-date with what is happening with her mother's condition.

While my friend's solution may not work for everyone, it identifies an important point: there are no fast rules for providing care for an aging parent. Knowing your own limits is the perfect place to start looking for solutions to meet care needs. Individual limits may be distance, time, psychological health or other commitments. These limits are unique to the individual, hence will be different for all the adult children in a family.

*It Isn't Fair*

Family dysfunction is the material of films, books and mental health problems. Our relationships with our parents and siblings are going to impact on future care plans for a dependent parent. An individual who visits a sick parent every day and takes on numerous domestic tasks while visiting may resent their sibling who visits on Sunday morning for an hour of tea and gossip - especially if the parent obviously looks forward to these Sunday visits. Yes, it isn't fair.

My maternal grandmother had many expectations about what her daughters should do during a visit, but when one of her sons popped by she sat back and enjoyed the visit without making any demands. Similarly, my absent father was regularly referred to as the 'favourite son' by my paternal grandmother as her dementia progressed, even though she received a daily visit from one of her three remaining sons.

At this stage a quick mention of in-laws in required. Throughout history the role of caring for aging in-laws has often dropped into the lap of the eldest daughter-in-law, most obviously in daughterless families in Asian countries. Cultural expectations and gender-based roles may seem to force you into this role, but the choice is still for the individual (daughter-in-law) to make.

## Team Plan

So what is the solution? When there is more than one adult child in a family, and especially if one or more family members does not live in the same town/country/continent as an aging parent who needs help – the best plan of action is to nominate a family manager. The nomination of a family manager is often done at the time when the parent's independence levels falter and help is needed on a regular basis.

*The family manager or family liaison person - if you find that title comes with an uncomfortable, but unintended, line of authority – is the person who:*

- has the best relationship with the siblings,
- is available to be the contact person for medical and health care services,
- is generally able to visit the parent on a regular basis, and most importantly,
- is level-headed and able to remain calm in times of stress.

For those of us who live far away, the family manager is the person we rely on to provide us with up-to-date information about our parent's health status including changes in care plans and care requirements.

Scheduling a weekly catch-up call or email with the family manager has the dual role of giving your support to the family manager while creating an opportunity to be involved in the care plan by having your questions and concerns for health workers relayed, should you not be able to contact the health professionals directly.

Most important: make sure that the family manager knows that you appreciate that they have taken on this difficult role in the family.

## Spousal Caregivers – 'Till Death Do Us Part'

As a young nurse trainee straight out of high school, I was assigned an 80-year-old woman, admitted to hospital because she was dying. The lady entered the hospital two weeks after the death of her husband of 50+ years. Her medical file was light on details: no sudden illnesses, chronic diseases or obvious causes resulting in her becoming bedridden and time-limited.

Understanding what was happening with this lady was beyond me. As way of explanation, the charge nurse told me that the woman wanted to die. That after her husband (who had been sick with cancer for almost a year) died, she ran out of reasons to live and was now willing herself to die.

As I gave her a bed-bath and changed her sheets, I tried to persuade the woman that there were many good reasons to be alive. Her eyes remained vacant and her lack of words told me that she was unconvinced by my arguments and determined in her own plan of action. She died on her fifth day in the hospital. Being young and inexperienced in most life matters this rendered me incapable of understanding her lust for death.

"Till death do us part" is part of a marriage vow originating from the Book of Common Prayer first published in 1549, still repeated in many wedding ceremonies conducted in the English speaking world. Rising divorce figures clearly indicate that an increasing number of couples are not taking this vow seriously, yet there remains a significant group of older adults able to legitimately celebrate 30, 40, 50 or even 60 years of marriage.

Getting old with someone you love is a popular romantic notion intrinsic in all societies. Generally over time romance diminishes and is replaced by more practical considerations like jobs, mortgages, children, vacations, aging parents etc. For better or worse, enduring partner projects are the things that glue many marriages together.

Increasing age comes with an escalating probability of illness and disability – often resulting in one partner taking on the role of caregiver for their ailing spouse. With most chronic illnesses, like dementia, this role can extend for years becoming heavier as the disease progresses.

Spousal caregivers frequently conceal their exhaustion and difficulties, not wanting to admit defeat by asking for help to look after their partners. This can cause stress that negatively impacts on the caregiver's health and ultimately leads to caregiver burnout.

Assessment of an in-home care situation with older couples is difficult for families and professionals alike. Family members are often blind to what is happening in their parent's home. They may believe that everything is okay and that their ill parent is having a rare 'bad day' when they visit or is unable to speak to them on the phone.

Health professionals may be denied entry into the home and distracted from the truth by cancelled appointments and assertions that everything is fine. The threat of separation by hospitalization or admission to residential care is a source of great anxiety for many older couples – as is the fear of being left alone.

Ironically, accepting the help that is available can often extend the time a chronically sick person can be managed within the home environment. For a spouse, accepting help can mean taking a well needed respite break – whether for a few hours or a few weeks. A good example is that of the many dementia sufferers exhibiting nocturnal sleeping disturbances, often waking caregivers with loud rummaging through drawers and wardrobes. Caregivers quickly become exhausted when their own night's sleep patterns are disrupted.

Providing a caregiver a few hours to sleep, relax, go to the movies, drink coffee with a friend, take a walk, whatever the person needs to do in order to replenish themselves is not a luxury – but a necessity. It helps them to maintain perspective and attachment to the world going on outside the home that holds them, albeit willingly, inside caring for their partner.

---

Ana McGinley

Home care services, support groups, older adult respite care programs (day and longer term), informal help from family and friends – are all options available to support older adults caring or being cared for within their own home. While little can be done to lighten or remove the feelings of loss and sadness at seeing a life partner suffering due to illness, we can help to ease the daily burden of care by encouraging older couples to accept the services available to them.

Most importantly, supporting the individuals, rather than seeing the couple as a single unit, will promote an individual acceptance of the situation from their own personal perspective and relieve the unreasonable expectation of "till death do us part."

# Communication

- Use the technology
- Holidays and home visits
- Visits when your parent lives in an aged care facility

> "It is not distance that keeps people apart, but lack of communication"
> (Anon)

I was a kid of the 70s. Definitely not a love child with parents into weed and flowers – but a child of immigrant parents living in a small Australian town. A weekday highlight was the sound of the postman approaching on his red motorbike, with the chance that he was carrying letters or postcards sent by my Dutch grandparents. I counted on the fact that they always remembered to send a postcard on my birthday, that I acknowledged with a return thank you card. Sometimes they sent a Christmas parcel filled with small toys and strange confectionary that looked like licorice but tasted like salty sick.

My relationship with my paternal grandparents was special. They visited us twice during my childhood, yet due to my young age I was unable to recall either visit. Instead, for me at least, the closeness came from the regular contact by post. I knew that I was important to them, even if they weren't around to babysit me like all the other grandparents in town.

As an adult I continued to send and receive cards from my grandmother. By then my grandfather had died (when I was a teenager) and she had moved to a retirement facility that offered additional services if and when needed. I visited her whenever I travelled to Europe.

The last time was when she was in her late 80s and had a moderate level of dementia. Her memory was shot and she needed daily help from staff and family members. She couldn't remember who I was, yet she enjoyed spending a few hours chatting and showing me her collection of photographs pointing out her grand-daughter (me). She also showed me her box of postcards, addressed and written to me and other family members living in Australia but not mailed. We had always been in her thoughts, even when her ability to get to the post office was lost.

Distance and dementia are a complicated duo. Decades have passed since I first spat out that disgusting Dutch salty licorice. The postman still has a job in most countries, although his bags are generally filled with bills and mail most people are not too excited at receiving. Keeping in touch with friends and family who live at a distance has changed. Personal letters and expensive long distance phone calls have become a memory from the past. Our means of communicating with one another has been transformed by technology – abandoning anyone resisting the conversion. As Bob Dylan has sung many times: "For The Times They Are A-Changing."

Technology has made keeping in contact with people around the world easy. My own children are in constant contact with their friends, both in the neighbourhood and around the world, via free phone apps like WhatsApp and Facetime. The hour-long late night telephone conversations of my teens, that drove my parents crazy, are not an issue in my own family of lounging teenagers. Companies schedule meetings with some attendees participating virtually via their computer screens from remote offices and cafes around the world. Friends follow one another's lives on blogs, Facebook, Instagram, Snapchat – rarely receiving a personal communication meant only for their eyes.

## Use the Technology

Distance does not need to be the demise of relationships. Being able to send an instant message, a short email, a photo, tagging someone on Facebook, or sending a link to an article about a topic they are interested in - are all things that take almost no time yet let the person know you are thinking about them

Scheduling a weekly Skype call with parents and grandparents is an ideal way to keep in regular contact. Grandchildren can share the highlights of their week.

Practical issues, like health care treatment plans and holiday arrangements, can be discussed at length. Family members can remain actively involved in one another's lives without being physically in the same house.

For families where all members are computer literate and enthusiastic, technology has made distant relationships – closer.

Yet not everyone has made the move. My mother has never used a computer. We have begged her to take a basic course on using the Internet to send/receive emails and make Skype video calls so that she can make contact whenever she wants - but she has always refused. I suspect she hopes the Internet is a fad that will disappear one day, like cassette players and men with perms.

For older people like my mum who have not embraced the Internet and mobile telephones, maintaining contact will take more time, effort and planning. I have a good friend who would record herself reading books and then send the recordings to her mother who was often bedridden due to her cancer treatments. Weekly telephone conversations, cards on birthdays and special events, letters with photos and drawings from grandchildren, holiday postcards – again, all signals to parents/grandparents that you are thinking of them and making the effort to keep in touch.

*Something Worth Considering Before You Head Out to Upgrade Your Parent's Computer System…*

Here is an observation from both my own family and from my husband's family. My father and mother-in-law were competent computer users for at least 15years. Although my father is about five years younger than my mother-in-law he began having problems with sending and opening emails about five years ago. My mother-in-law often seems to have computer problems that limit her contact.

In both families the response has been to buy them newer, more compact computers (iPads, Kindles, iPhones). My siblings and in-laws really believe that giving a gift of the newest technology is going to solve the problem of communication and make the person more reliably accessible to family. Not true. My father now needs my sister to come and help him find his emails and to send any emails he has written that are sitting in his draft mail. My sister must also set up any Skype calls that he is involved in.

My mother-in-law continues to prefer to call the home phone, even if she is using Skype. Sometimes she will send a text message or like a photo on Facebook – but I suspect that this is when she is with family who are able to remind her how to find these applications on her devices. It is not that she can't use the Internet, it's more that remembering all the 'simpler' steps that each piece of new technology introduces or changes is a pain in the neck and open to many errors. It is for me, at least.

## Holidays and Home Visits

Being able to spend physical time with aging parents is going to depend on distance, finances, desire and available free time. Specifically, many expats have faced budget cuts removing previously funded annual family holidays to the employee's country of origin from their employment contracts. As a result, many expat families are no longer able to afford annual trips home to visit aging relatives.

Similarly if families have independently moved seeking better work, study or lifestyle options their travel budget may be reduced by the expenses of relocation.

Alternative options to making a "home" holiday trip to visit a parent every year include making plans to visit once every 2-5 years; contributing to the cost of parents coming to visit; or choosing mid-way holiday destinations with both parties sharing the costs of travelling only half the distance.

## Visits When Your Parent Lives in an Aged Care Facility

If your parent is moved to an aged care facility, a home trip may involve a daily visit where you spend time together either within their room, or in a quiet common area like a garden. Being able to take your parent away from the facility will be appreciated by parents who are physically capable of an outing – be it via a car journey, or, a walk through the neighbourhood in a wheelchair. Visits should be kept to a few hours, or shorter if your parent tires easily.

For people with parents who have a dementia, visits can be frustrating or sad experiences especially if your parent doesn't recognize you. It is important to anticipate how you will feel if this does occur, as being unable to recognize adult children is common in people with dementia. In this situation, the visit you make should be aimed at providing a pleasant social occasion with your parent. A chance to talk, reminisce and feel valued. I recommend using old photographs to initiate a conversation and increase the chances of connecting with your parent. These visits can be very difficult for adult children.

Use the visit to check that your parent is having all their needs adequately met by the facility. Do they look like they are receiving sufficient nutrition? Are they clean? Is the facility, and their room, well maintained? Is your parent being treated respectfully? What does your parent do during the day? Are they encouraged to join in the activities being offered? Take it upon yourself to find out about the care your parent actually receives at the facility and if there is anything that would improve the quality of their daily life. Be that annoying relative. You owe it to your parent.

# Common Chronic Diseases Of The Elderly

- Dementia
- Heart Disease
- Stroke
- Cancer
- Arthritis
- Multi-mix of Problems

Consider the top five causes on death in Britain's over-65 population (2012): heart disease, lung cancer, emphysema/bronchitis, cerebrovascular disease (stroke), dementia (think Alzheimer's disease). All five are classified as chronic illnesses because the person lives with a deteriorating condition from the time of diagnosis until they die – a process that could take weeks, months or years. (UK Office of National Statistics, 2013)

If chronic diseases were numbers on a bingo card, my father would be close to putting down his fat felt pen and yelling out to claim his frozen chickens (being that he lives in Australia – replace with box of chocolates if this is an unfamiliar bingo reference). In the past five years he has been diagnosed with diabetes, arthritis, early dementia – and hospitalized on three occasions following a heart attack and a couple of trans ischemic attacks (commonly referred to as mini-strokes).

At 76, he too remains the same person he always was, except that he is depressed and frustrated by feelings of being vulnerable and dependent. He was a world traveller and expat with a love of meeting people from different cultures. For him the difference in his current lifestyle choices is caused by the health problems that currently threaten even his ability to drive his car around his local neighbourhood.

So where is this leading? The point I want to make is that aging is a natural part of life. Being old does not mean being reliant on others. Being sick often makes all of us, regardless of age, dependent, albeit generally only on a temporary basis. Being old and debilitated by a chronic illness is the combination most likely to result in a need for help over a longer period of time.

Further, the *impact* of a new health problem directly correlates to how the person was functioning prior to this new problem. Hence, if the person already has existing health problems (like chronic pain and lack of mobility due to arthritis) and then suffers a stroke – the chances of making a full recovery are severely reduced and the probability that informal (from family and friends) and formal help (paid services) will be required is high.

The next section explains the five most common chronic health problems affecting older adults. A heart attack and a stroke are serious and sudden insults caused by chronic (long-standing) diseases. All diseases discussed generally result in a need for assistance over time to help the person maintain a level of independence.

(And yes I acknowledge that there is a long list of other debilitating diseases like Parkinson's Disease, late onset

Schizophrenia, Macular Degeneration that cause similar levels of dependency but could not be covered in detail in this short guide.)

## Identifying the Main Health Problems

*Dementia*

> Dementia is a general term for a decline in mental ability severe enough to interfere with a daily life. Memory loss is an example. Alzheimer's is the most common type of dementia.
> (Alzheimer's Association 2015)

Other types of dementia include Vascular Dementia; Lewy body Dementia; Creutzfeldt-Jakob Disease; Frontotemporal Dementia; and dementias that come as part of the package of other diseases like Parkinson's Disease, AIDS, and Huntington's Disease. Lots of names yet a formal diagnosis of the type of dementia remains a technical formality based on expensive screening and longitudinal data collection, especially in a time when the cure for all dementing illnesses remains non-existent.

In short, here is the deal with dementia: with increased age comes increased risk of dementia, especially Alzheimer's disease. Recent figures from America indicate that 4% of people under the age of 65 are diagnosed with dementia, with many people in this group having a family history of early diagnosis, and/or strong genetic markers for the disease. Jump ahead to the 65-75 year old group, and the number increases to 15%. The scary part is yet to come. For people in the 75-84 year old group, the chance of being diagnosed with dementia has almost tripled to 44% (Alzheimers.net 2015). This figure comes with a gentle reminder that being forgetful is not a part of general aging, only a popular and somewhat old-fashioned stereotype.

Dementia is a disease that slowly debilitates the person. The prognosis of the disease depends on age and pre-existing health problems at the time of diagnosis. This means that someone diagnosed with Alzheimer's disease as a 70-year-old, could expect to live longer than someone diagnosed as an 85-year-old – simply based on general life expectancy rates. The disease will also have greater repercussions on the person's daily life if they are younger and still actively involved in the work force, community, raising children or grandchildren, or the activities that they enjoy.

Dementia affects more than a person's memory. It robs the person of their ability to participate in social occasions, to complete familiar tasks, to recognize friends and family members, to orientate themselves in familiar places, and to be self-reliant.

Dementia is a devastating disease for the person and for the family. Worldwide, care of people with dementia is mostly provided within the home by family members, with formal services coming in later in the disease progression to assist with heavier tasks and to provide some respite to exhausted caregivers. Looking after someone with dementia is difficult, with more than 60% of family caregivers showing high levels of stress resulting from this role.

*Heart Disease*

Heart disease holds the unenviable international title of being the number one cause of death – killing more than seven million people each year.

In simple terms heart disease, often referred to as coronary artery disease or ischemic heart disease, occurs when the arteries leading to the heart become narrowed or blocked by deposits of fatty plaques. These plaques make it harder for the heart to pump blood around the body. Too much pressure on the heart from blocked arteries causes a heart attack. (National Heart, Lung & Blood Institute 2015)

Heart disease hits both men and women of all ethnicities. Considered a lifestyle disease, if an early diagnosis is made and strict lifestyle changes adhered to, the risk of heart disease progressing to a fatal heart attack can be significantly reduced. (Medicine Net 2015)

It sounds easy until you consider the risk factors: lack of exercise, poor diet, high blood pressure, excessive alcohol, smoking, high blood pressure, high cholesterol, diabetes, obesity and depression. (Maier 2014) If you are 75, overweight, unable to mobilize freely due to arthritis in your hips and knees – then chances are that you are going to struggle to lose adequate weight to reduce your cholesterol and blood pressure. Realizing that you are unable to follow the treatment plan might make you feel depressed and in need of few drinks every day. Not everyone balks at the challenge of prevention and treatment via lifestyle changes – but many find the reality too difficult to follow and opt for medication.

*Strokes (Cerebral Vascular Accident)*

*A stroke occurs when the blood supply to the brain is interrupted. There are two ways that his can happen:*

- an artery becomes blocked (ischemic stroke), or,
- an artery bursts (a haemorrhagic stroke).

In both instances a section of the brain dies (brain infarct) due to lack of oxygen and nutrients.

Every four minutes an American dies, suffering a stroke. This is mind-blowing especially as, similar to heart disease, stroke prevention is about leading a healthy lifestyle. The same risk factors apply: poor diet, smoking, excessive alcohol, high blood pressure, lack of exercise, obesity and high cholesterol. In addition being male, old and having a family history of stroke are all factors that increase the risk of having a stroke. Reading the fine print, additional risk factors include: diabetes, irregular pulse, fibromuscular dysplasia – and having a history of TIAs (mini-strokes). (CDC 2015)

Although suffering a stroke may be the first sign of an underlying health problem, many people admit to having a history of prior health struggles due to high blood pressure and poor circulation, often directly related to the long term effects of a poor diet and limited mobility.

More significantly is the impact on health and independence that a non-fatal stroke can have. Recent figures coming out of Australia show that some 65% of people who survive a stroke, end up living with a disability and require help to carry out their daily living activities. Stroke-related disabilities include impediments in walking, talking, eating, bathing and dressing. (Stroke Foundation 2015)

*Cancer*

Not just for older people, cancer (malignant neoplasms) is not fussy about gender, age, or ethnic background. Yet another morbid 2014 statistic shows that 1600 Americans die each day from cancer, predominantly lung, colon, breast and prostrate cancer. In the same year, about 1.6million people received a new cancer diagnosis.(Science Daily 2014) Admittedly, the United States is a big place, but these figures mean that everyone knows someone who has cancer.

Cancer Research UK (n.d) advise that four out of ten cancers can be prevented by maintaining a healthy weight, eating a healthy diet (high fibre diet, 5-6 servings of fruit/veg, less red meat, less processed food, less salt); not smoking; less alcohol, being active, and being 'sun smart'. Further recommendations include breastfeeding; avoiding workplace hazards like asbestos; and, minimizing exposure to radiation.

Caring for someone with cancer can be physically and emotionally draining, often necessitating professional care to help with pain management. Practical help, like shopping and cleaning, is often required during radiation and chemotherapy treatments, while nursing care may be needed to help with bathing, wound dressings and monitoring. Again, the majority of care takes place in the home, at least until the person requires an admission to hospital or hospice at the final stages of the disease.

*Arthritis*

With over a 100 different types of arthritis, this brief explanation will be limited to the most commonly occurring arthritis diagnosed in older adults: Osteoarthritis and Rheumatoid Arthritis.

Osteoarthritis is a degenerative joint disease that develops after trauma or infection to the joint, and with aging of a joint that has experienced considerable usage - like hands, feet, wrists, back, hips and knees. Osteoarthritis causes pain during movement and in later years can result in continuous pain in the area.

Rheumatoid Arthritis mainly affects the joints in the fingers, wrists, elbows and knees. This disorder sees the body's immune system attacking the joint lining and cartilage, causing the bones to rub together, often damaging the bones themselves. (Arthritis 2015)

There is no known cure for either osteoarthritis or rheumatoid arthritis. Treatment begins with pain relief medications as both conditions can give the person considerable discomfort either when moving or being still. Physiotherapy is often recommended – with aqua-therapy being a popular treatment plan given by some specialists. Losing weight, exercising and joint replacements are included in the list of recommendations.

In the UK, there are an estimated 10 million people afflicted by arthritis. Around 65% of these people report being unable to even make themselves a cup of tea when their pain is peaking. (Arthritis Care 2015)

Often it is the home environment that needs to be modified to make life easier for the person with arthritis. Less stairs, showers instead of baths, being wheelchair accessible, automatic rather than manual kitchen tools (like electric can openers) – are all changes that can help the person maintain independence.

*Multiple Health Problems*

Reading the medical files for hospital patients over the age of 65 generally makes for a long read. Frequently older patients have a multitude of health complaints that necessitate referral to and assessment by a variety of specialists. These specialists tend to work independent of one another, and prescribe medications and treatment plans to deal with a specific complaint without consultation with specialists treating other parts of the patient's body.

Human bodies are like cars. Old bodies need to be treated with care to ensure longevity. Identifying one problem can often open the door hiding another health problem that has been unwittingly managed without being recognized. Just like a beautiful old car heading to the garage because a little smoke is blowing out from under the hood. Chances are it is going to need more than just an oil change.

In an ideal world, all people over the age of 65 would have their health care managed by a specialist team. The team would be experts in total body management of the older person, and have in depth knowledge about what the chemical implications of taking handfuls of different medications has on an aging body. They would consider the feasibility of recommending exercise programs to lose weight when the person is in constant pain from arthritis – and come up with more appropriate options. The team would be up-to-date on the available services in the community and refer to these services accordingly – aware that family members want to do their best to help but are often limited by their own families, or jobs, or a distance of 15,000kms….

*Quick disclaimer: I do not advocate going medication free, but I do believe that many additional health complaints in older people (including dizziness, falls, and intestinal complaints) are related to the chemical reactions that happen when you put a handful of different medications together in an acid environment like your stomach. Discuss this possibility with your parent's doctor.*

# Safety Within the Home

- Assessing safety in the home
- Falls
- Fires
- Inadequate nutrition
- Alcohol abuse
- Medication-related problems
- Social isolation and loneliness
- How to help
- Making it simple

## Assessing Safety in the Home

Safety within the home becomes a real issue as people age. Increased dangers come with decreased mobility, sensory deficits, dementia and medications.

Consider how being unable to smell a pan burning on the stove can quickly become a fire risk. Slipping in the shower, tripping over the cat, or forgetting that the iron is lying flat on the ironing board – can all result in serious injuries or potential death of an older person especially if they are living alone.

There are things that you can do to maximize safety and reduce risks that your parent may encounter in their everyday home lives. This can be done during a longer visit with your parent. It can also be something that family members or friends who live in the vicinity are asked to monitor over a longer period.

The first step will be to assess what the potential dangers are. To make this assessment you need to be with your parent in their home over a period of time. You need to be "a visitor", capable of resisting your urge to help with the tasks that your parent is completing with difficulty.

The aim of the assessment is to watch your parent completing tasks *inconspicuously* to check whether they are exposing themselves to possible safety risks. Activities should include cooking, washing, vacuuming, gardening, shopping – things they do everyday. In addition, consider how they are mobilizing in their home. Do they need to grab onto furniture and walls to maintain their balance? Can they easily get in and out chairs, bed and the bath? After a few days, you should have some idea about what tasks are now providing a challenge or safety risk to your parent.

For parents who are in hospital, you can request that the occupational therapist come to the home and assess your parent in their own environment. If your parent is at home and under the care of a community-based health care team, the case manager should be contacted if you have some safety concerns. Request that the case manager arrange for an occupational therapist to visit.

> "Hindsight is a wonderful thing but foresight is better, especially when it comes to saving life, or some pain"
> William Blake

## Falls

My family and I are postural droppers. We frequently have someone standing too fast, and woozily grabbing onto the closest object to stop from crashing to the ground. The main casualty is my 13-year-old son, who has stretched to almost two metres in the past year. He has hit the ground a few times painting the walls and floors with whatever was in his breakfast bowl. His height means that his standing blood pressure needs a little more time to equalize. Luckily we have a busy house with many people available to help should you be sprawled on the ground.

Postural hypotension is common in older people and places them at risk of falling and sustaining serious injuries if hitting their heads or twisting their limbs. Living alone increases the risk that injuries may result in extended suffering until the person is discovered. It may sound dramatic – yet it happens frequently enough for companies that sell personal alarms to have flourishing businesses.

Seeing an older person fall is traumatic. It isn't the same experience of seeing a toddler falling over, noisily getting back on their feet to bounce on to their next fall.

An older person who has fallen over won't be bouncing back up. In fact many falls result in an admission to hospital and are often the precursor to an early demise.

Studies have found that a third of all people in the over 65 age group sustain at least one fall a year. Falls are the major cause of both fatal and non-fatal injuries in the elderly. Most fractures (hips, legs, arms, spine, hand) in this group are due to a fall. Yet even when fractures have not occurred, many people develop a fear of falling that limits their activities and reduces their mobility and physical fitness. (CDC 2015)

*Falls in the elderly can often be prevented by:*

- Reducing trip hazards and making the home environment user-friendly – that is, matching your parent's current needs and abilities. This includes removing rugs, clutter, adding grab bars to bathrooms and toilets, removing objects from high shelves, and improving lighting.
- Asking doctors to check whether dizziness, drowsiness and low blood pressure are side effects of prescribed medications– and if possible to refrain from prescribing these medications to your parent.

- Retesting of eyesight to check that visual deficits aren't increasing the risk of tripping or misjudging distances.
- Encouraging your parent to regularly partake in exercise programs that improve balance and core strength. If your parent is in a rehabilitation program following a stroke or due to arthritis, specifically ask the physiotherapist to assess their balance.

## Fires

As with all homes, especially older houses, the risk of fires due to faulty electrical problems is always a possibility. Many fires started in the kitchen are due to food being forgotten and left cooking on the stove; or with long sleeves catching fire; or with being unable to put out a fire that starts in a pan. Similarly forgetting to turn off the iron or toaster (especially older models) can result in a fire risk. Yet the principal fire hazard to older people is that of smoking. Falling asleep with a cigarette in your hand can quickly become disastrous.

Death or serious injury from home fires in the elderly is increased due to reduced sensory input especially smell, reduced decision-making ability (due to dementia or some medications), and reduced mobility.

*Hence:*

- Check fire alarms are in place and working and nominate someone to change batteries regularly.
- Replace or check old appliances to minimize the risk that they will start a fire if forgotten. For example many modern irons and stoves turn themselves off if their sensors detect no movement for a few minutes.
- Is there a fire extinguisher in the home? Can your parent use it? Is there a fire escape route that is regularly checked with your parent?
- Is the phone number for the fire department (ambulance and police) known? Can it be programmed into the home telephone?
- How can fire risks be minimized if your parent smokes? Can their smoking habit be restricted to outside the home? Can fire resistant fabrics be used on sofas, chairs, beds and for curtains?

## Inadequate Nutrition

In most cultures the sharing of a meal has high social value. Family dinners are not restricted to festive occasions, they are an intrinsic part of family life often extended to include friends, acquaintances and business associates. Mealtimes are times of conversation, bonding and updating. At times, it can also be the setting for arguments, tears, shouting and embarrassing drunken faux pas.

A 72-year-old friend recently confessed that she would never go into a restaurant alone and order a meal. This lady is extremely social and is out of the house most days and evenings enjoying her various commitments. She admits to a lack of interest in cooking, although her eating schedule remains semi-regular as she eats many meals at home with her husband.

But what would happen if she was alone at home, and her urge to be away from her loneliness meant skipping food preparation and meals? Would she forgo meals? This is a familiar scenario for older people, who often find it too much effort to bother cooking for one.

In my family the older people become the more their cooking deteriorates. In general they continue to appreciate delicious, well-prepared meals, yet their ability and enthusiasm to construct these meals disappears.

A few decades ago, my maternal grandmother regularly spent hours in her kitchen preparing food for her extended family, including the slaughter of rabbits for a traditional Maltese stew. Her dishes always appreciated by her adult children, horrified some grandchildren wise enough to equate the missing bunnies with the funny tasting chicken. In her later years she seemed content to drink large glasses of milky tea that she soaked plain cookies in, or to eat the same boring soup for days on end. Both these dishes seem to be very popular with older people who live alone – because they are easy to prepare and soft to chew.

My mother-in-law who still whips up a wonderful dinner party if the need arises, reports that she likes to freeze leftover salad that she later turns into a single serving of soup. I am not 100% certain of this, but my guess would be reheated frozen lettuce soup has a negative nutritional value. Living alone detrimentally affects your health when the effort to prepare healthy, nutritious food for one person is too much hassle. My own diet of instant noodles, instant coffee and peanut butter toast in my cash-strapped student days added little to my energy levels and positive attitude.

Maintaining a good diet is important in all age groups. An older body needs nutritious food to maintain itself and to prevent further health problems. The easiest example to illustrate this point is *constipation.* An estimated 50% of people over the age of 65 living at home suffer from constipation. For people living in residential care facilities this percentage increases to 74%. (Rao &Jorge 2010) Reducing the intake of fruits, vegetables, water and high-fiber foods impacts on the digestive system and often results in constipation. It can be a side effect of medications, a depressed mood, motor skill problems or the result of a lack of exercise. People who have had a stroke or diabetes commonly suffer from constipation.

Not so nice to think about, yet untreated constipation can result in fecal impaction and fecal incontinence. One study estimates that 40% of elderly patients in UK hospitals suffer from fecal obstruction – which can cause severe confusion, intestinal obstruction, and bowel perforation in older adults. (Rao & Jorge 2010)

As if there wasn't enough going on for the person admitted to hospital.

How can you help to ensure your parent is eating an adequate diet? Arranging to have someone come and share a meal with your parent every few days has obvious nutritional and social benefits. This can be a family member, neighbour, friend or volunteer. It can take place at your parent's home, a café/restaurant/social club, the house of the dining partner – or outside as a picnic or barbeque. Some families have a roster of eating partners: people who will visit and eat with their parent each night, leaving the day visits to be spontaneous events.

Home delivered meal services may also be an appropriate solution to ensuring an adequate nutritional intake. Even better a weekly delivery of a meal from your parent's favourite restaurant can help encourage them to eat.

## Alcohol Abuse

Drinking too much alcohol on a regular basis is going to become problematic for individuals in every age group. Problems are exacerbated in the elderly because they are at higher risk of serious injuries (due to falls) that they will not recover quickly from. Adding alcohol to their regime of medications won't make the medications work better, and may even negate what the medication is prescribed for. The combination of alcohol and medications may even result in the introduction of new health complaints.

Below is a list of physical and behavioral changes that could be attributed to alcohol abuse in an older adult (Miller 1993). This list was compiled by Nancy Winialski, the director of a chemical dependency program at Gaylord Hospital in Wallingford, familiar with older adults who are admitted to the program:

- Frequent falls or an automobile accident
- Forgetfulness
- Problems like ulcers, inflammation of the stomach or pancreas, liver disease and abnormally high blood pressure
- Unexpected mood swings
- Slurred speech
- Frequent drowsiness
- A desire to be alone more than usual
- Changes in daily routine; illogical explanations for changes in behavior

- Failure to keep appointments

It would be barbaric to recommend total abstinence from alcohol for older people. I actually believe that a daily glass of wine, sherry, beer or whatever is your drink-of-choice is one of life's pleasures that should be continued to the end. My own kids have already been prepped to bring me a daily cup of real espresso coffee and a glass of merlot – should I one day move into an aged care facility. It is a quality of life issue recognized by some shrewd facility owners who offer the extra paid service of a glass of wine to residents with their evening meal.

Many years ago I met an older woman living alone in a barred up flat in the suburbs of Sydney. She had never married and had no identifiable friends or family. She was a difficult woman to meet as she refused to let hospital staff into her home. This lady had a diagnosis of "senile squalor", which translates as a condition where the person compulsively fills their home with old paper, plastic containers, everything they have collected over many years and are unwilling to throw away. This lady also showed symptoms of dementia.

After an admission to hospital, she was discharged to a hostel (low care facility), where she had her own room and bathroom, but was otherwise expected to socialize with the other residents. This was problematic for her. She was able to deal with one-on-one interactions but the group dynamic was not for her.

What she actually wanted to do was to sit in her room with her things, watch her television, and enjoy a glass or two of sherry (which she would beg me to go and buy for her). Considering that she had been moved from her home to a care facility where she was forced to live with strangers, her behavior seemed well within normal boundaries. It is also how I would envisage myself in the same situation. We have some weird expectations that old people will behave in ways that we would never agree to ourselves.

## Medication-Related Problems

The following quote is from Karen Hitchcock, an Australian doctor who has worked with elderly patients in some of the country's major teaching hospitals.

> The elderly are inappropriately prescribed far too many drugs. If we follow international treatment guidelines for each disease in the average frail patient on my ward, they receive upwards of twelve drugs a day that need to be taken at five different times of day with the risk of at least ten serious adverse effects. Many elderly patients come to hospital with these kinds of medication regimens. Twenty to thirty per cent of all hospital admissions in those over the age of sixty-five are related to illness directly caused by their prescribed medications.
>
> (Hitchcock 2015 p41)

Many older people swallow prescribed pills by the handful. About six months ago, my father reported that he was taking 16 tablets per day, excluding vitamins. This is not unusual. In my work I have encountered people prescribed and ingesting twice that number of tablets daily without question.

Repairing the damage caused by too many tablets on aging bodies fills a significant part of the health care service provided by a geriatrician. Many times a geriatrician will reduce the list of medications due to side effects. Medications may even be replaced by alternatives that can be combined with other essential medications. Yet this is only part of the problem.

The second concern with prescription medications is whether the correct dose is being taken at the recommended time during the day. This problem can be lessened with the use of a dosage box - a segmented box where tablets are sorted according to the day and time they need to be taken. Often it is possible to arrange for the local chemist or a community health nurse, to fill the box correctly.

## Social Isolation & Loneliness

For me it is difficult to image what waking to quietness is like as I am constantly surrounded by noisy kids, demanding pets, music machines and friendly neighbours. Even my appliances seem to have their own loud, demanding language. Although my initial thought is about the peace that must come with waking alone everyday, I readily acknowledge that the fabric of our lives is sewn together by the people in it. We rely on other people to give the feedback needed to maintain our own self-identity. Looking in the mirror is not enough to tell us who we are.

Social isolation can lead to depression. According to the 2012 figures from the Australian Bureau of Statistics, 37% of all suicides were carried out by men in the over 85s age group – a figure triple the national suicide rate for all age groups. (ABC News 2014) What a tragedy!

Experts claim that the increased rate of suicide in this age group is due to grief and loss. That is, by the time a person reaches the grand age of 85, it is common to have experienced the deaths of a spouse, family members, and friends. He/she has confronted a loss of self-identity that often emerges in the post retirement years.

He/she may be depressed by impairments and discomfort caused by acute and chronic diseases. Being alone, without the presence of other people to provide distraction from one's reality, could easily lead to depression and introduce doubt about the value of one's own life.

## How to Help

Increasing regular social activities will generally decrease loneliness and improve mood. Social activities have the added benefit of connecting, or reconnecting, your parent to their local community. This is essential when there is an absence of family members living close by.

Discuss possibilities with your parent. What would they like to do?

Research what social activities are available for isolated older people in the local area. Contact hospital social workers; aged care community liaison person at the local government office; aged care advocacy service, or community health service staff – requesting information and advice. Look for options in local newspapers, libraries, and via Internet searches for "activities for older adults (town, city name)".

*As part of your search consider the following:*

- Is transport provided?
- Is lunch provided?
- Does the timing clash with other regular appointments (for example physiotherapy)
- Will there be any familiar faces at the activity for your parent?
- What is the cost involved?
- What is the daily program? Does it also involve regular outings?
- What are the other participants like? (Notably, if many of the other participants have a dementia and your parent does not, this is not going to be appropriate)
- Is there a monitoring service – that is, will someone contact you if they have concerns about your parent?

Ideally, the next step is to accompany your parent to the activity, so that you can assess whether it is a good fit for them. This can happen during a visit with your parent.

Expect some resistance to joining a new group, as this reluctance to join a group of strangers is something we all have. Having direct experience of the social group gives a better link to your future, perhaps long-distance, conversations.

If you are unable to arrange social activities in person, request that social workers (before they are discharged from hospital), or community health care staff, or informal contacts make the necessary arrangements for your parent.

Some people will simply refuse to join group activities outside the home. In this case, a weekly visitor to the home is recommended. Visitors can be family members, friends, neighbours, or volunteers from community groups. Ideally someone who can take your parent out of the home for a few hours, and is capable of assessing the emergence of new problems with cognition and mobility.

Services offering a daily phone call to isolated older people exist in many countries. One company that provides this service in Australia in the Red Cross – under the name: Telecross. Basically someone from the organization phones the person (or your parent) on a daily basis to check on their well-being. Similar services are available through volunteer groups and charity organizations around the world. If your parent lives somewhere that a phone service does not cover, you may be able to make private arrangements to have someone local call your parent each morning.

Finally, phone calls to your parent at regular times during the week, emails and text messages (if possible), and sending letters and frequent postcards will significantly reduce feelings of loneliness.

## Make it Simple

Talk with your parent about tasks that they have difficulties with. In most situations it is possible to ask or pay someone to take over these tasks on a regular basis. One example may be to arrange for a gardener to cut the grass and tidy the garden on a fortnightly basis. This means that your parent is still able to enjoy their garden, without seeing it as a burden to maintain.

Similarly arranging a cleaning service or asking a neighbour to help take out and bring in large rubbish bins as required – can make life easier for an aging parent.

Simplifying the home by having electric products that will turn themselves off if forgotten; lights with long-life bulbs; removing tripping hazards; and replacing old appliances with safe, simple to use appliances (Note: forget the remote control with a hundred options).

Recommend that your parent wear a personal alarm at all times, so that they can receive help if needed. It is a simple device that has saved many people who have suffered a heart attack, stroke or fall while being alone at home.

# Risks Outside The Home

- Dementia and wandering
- Driving
- Public transport
- Exploitation from strangers

Some years ago a geriatrician asked me to accompany him on a visit to an aged care facility. This request was remarkable, because it differed from the usual objective of assessing a specific individual, or providing support to family members. The request entailed speaking with management staff about providing adequate protection for residents with dementia, without comprising their individual dignity.

The facility was a secure unit – which means that entry and exit to the building required the tapping in of a security code that opened the doors. The goal being to keep residents locked inside the building for their own safety, deemed necessary as many residents suffered from dementia and had lost the ability to orient themselves to places.

In this particular facility there lived a gentleman – who had a moderate level of dementia and, seemingly, the cunning of a teenager. He escaped from the facility on numerous occasions. Each time he was discovered walking along the local shopping street by pedestrians concerned for his safety, after watching him cross a busy intersection.

Being responsible for his safety, the staff at the facility decided to solve this problem by pinning signs, identifying him as a resident of the facility and requesting his return, to the back of his clothing. As health professionals, we judged this solution to be demeaning to the man and helped staff find new solutions to ensure his safety.

## Dementia and Wandering

Wandering and getting lost because of an inability to recognize familiar surroundings or to remember where you are heading, is common in people with dementia. This behavior puts them at a safety risk and creates stress for the person and their families.

It is often the impetus leading to the person being moved into a dementia care facility.

Spousal caregivers lock doors and windows to keep the person inside the house and prevent them from leaving and becoming lost. This safety measure is essential for people who wake during the night to rummage for lost items they believe to be located outside the house. As noted with the gentleman with the signs pinned on his clothing, predicting which skills remain intact when a person has dementia is difficult. This man was unable to dress himself, yet was capable of spying on family members as they typed in the security codes, and then use the code to escape from the facility.

Imagine losing someone or something, but being unable to remember that the person or item has been permanently removed. Imagine waking everyday with the strong need to find the person or the thing. Imagine how confusing it would be to be continually told that you are wrong, and that the person has died or the thing was disposed of long ago. I suggest that this would incur feelings of anger, disbelief, sadness - and loneliness. This is what happens with someone with dementia.

Safety measures for people with dementia:

- Ensure that they have identification on them at all times. This may involve having labels made with their name and a contact phone number – that are then sewn inside their clothing. Some people choose to have a bracelet made with the information. Relying on someone with dementia to carry a wallet or purse with them should they leave the home is insufficient.
- Make sure that you have a recent photo of the person – just in case they do go missing.
- Doors, windows and garden gates should be made secure, especially when people with dementia live above ground floor level. Keys need to be kept safe and out of temptation from the person.
- Just like everyone else, getting outside and releasing energy is healthy – and not doing so

every day can cause irritation, sleep problems and depression. For people with dementia, exercise during the day will help to regulate their body clocks to minimize nocturnal disturbances. For spousal caregivers – getting time outside without their partner with dementia is also crucial. This may mean finding someone to stay with the person for a few hours to relieve the caregiver.

## Driving

> I love driving behind old people. You can get so much done: Eat breakfast, lunch and dinner, read a book, write a book.
> (anonymous)

Stereotypes of old people driving cars are numerous, albeit always unflattering towards drivers who often have 40+ years of driving experience under their (seat)belts. While most of us wouldn't argue that decreased vision, hearing, and mobility are common factors of aging – it is the question of when these deficits make a person unsafe to drive that opens the quagmire of discussions on individual rights; community safety; isolation; adequate provision of public transport; town planning; home help services; family responsibility, and independence.

In many countries, people over a certain age (country specific) must agree to being reassessed by the driver's licensing authorities. If family members have sufficient concerns about the person driving before scheduled retesting, they may contact the family doctor. Based on this hearsay from family members and/or caregivers, the doctor can request an early reassessment or a revocation of their driving license.

This issue has recently arisen in my own family. My father who has numerous health problems, now including a diagnosis of early-stage dementia, has bumped his car into two parked cars at my brother's home. I have three separate sibling accounts. My brother reports that my father is an unsafe driver and has contacted the doctor. One sister stated that the car he drives is too large for him to handle, and consequently he did not see the parked cars he knocked. My remaining sister has not had any recent experience of driving with our father, but based on his other health problems, feels that he shouldn't be driving.

Flipside: my father needs a car to get around in the rural town he lives in. He is unable to walk more than 100metres and public transport is not an option. His daily routine involves a drive to his local McDonalds for a morning coffee and then on to my brother's business – before driving home three hours later (total distance per day of 5km). The remainder of the day he sleeps or watches television.

Removal of his car and license will mean that he spends all day at home, dependent on my mother and siblings – who are busy with their own lives. He will loose the routine that gets him out of bed and into the community each day.

My father's story will sound familiar to many people. Naturally should he be an obvious risk to other drivers – and to himself – removing his license would be essential. But this is the sticking point. As with many older people in the early stages of chronic illnesses, like dementia, the disease progress slowly destroys skills and abilities.

His general practitioner and his physician have never been in a car with him, and must rely on the hearsay of family members reluctant to embarrass my father by complaining about his driving. The MMSE (Mini Mental State Exam – a set of 30 questions used to assess memory, language and attention) that is administered on each visit to the physician gives little indication of driver safety.

Yet a diagnosis is only a label with a likely path of prognosis. People need to be considered as individuals. Other health problems, especially with eyesight and hearing, need to be evaluated should driving safety be a concern. Safer alternatives should be implemented – for example, driving only familiar routes, only during daytime hours and in good weather, driving with someone else, and retesting.

Finally – considering how routines and social contacts outside the home can be maintained should the person no longer be able to drive is important in making the transition from being an independent driver to someone dependent on others to be where they want to be – a little easier to accept.

The issue of older drivers and road safety is not a laughing matter. Looking at fatality figures from Queensland, the Australian state where my parents live, 21% of the 2014 traffic related deaths in the state involved people over the age of 65. Of this number, about half were driving the car, 20% were passengers, 20% were pedestrians and the remaining victims were riding either a motorcycle or bicycle. (CARRS-Q 2015)

Overall, the rate of being in a car accident is less compared to the general population (and the number of drivers significantly decreases as age increases), yet the risk of being fatally injured is much higher than the norm.

*If you think your parent's driving is a safety issue…*

- When you visit – let your parent drive you. Pay attention to their driving and monitor your concerns over your visit. If you have concerns, discuss with your parent, family members and treating doctors.
- Ask to have an early driving assessment by local transport authorities.
- Check the car for bumps and scratches – and ask your parent about causes.

- Discuss other possible causes for driving difficulties with your parent and doctor. Poor vision and restricted mobility will negatively affect driving.
- Research options for transportation. Is public transport available and accessible to your parent? Could they use an electric bicycle, electric wheelchair or a mobility scooter – instead of a car to maintain their independence?
- For people with dementia, remembering that they are not allowed to drive can cause daily arguments for caregivers. Consider parking the car away from the house; changing the keys on the keychain; and disabling the car engine – to reduce the temptation to drive.

The main issue is safety – for your parent and other people on the roads and footpaths.

## Public Transport

Older people who are reliant on public transport to access their local community may require special consideration to reduce risks as they become less mobile. More time is needed to prevent rushing. Careful scheduling of appointments and plans that do not require catching buses, trains and trams during peak hours is recommended. If walking sticks, frames or other aides are used, making sure that that they do not become a falls risk when entering and exiting transport is definitely worth assessing. Often similar, lighter aides are available to use when the person is moving around outside the home environment.

## Exploitation by Strangers

Last week I was swindled by the chimney-sweeper I had booked to clean my chimneys. He sold me two tins of powder that I assumed were to be added to the burning wood, with the resultant smoke cleaning the residue in the chimneys.

I don't know much about fireplaces, and the slickness and speed of this particular gentleman (plus the conversation being conducted in a language I am not fluent in) clouded my judgment, turning me stupid as I took out my purse and handed over some money for this sucker product. My husband dared to laugh even as I confessed my foolery.

Charlatans continue to knock on our doors and call our telephones. Isolated older people are vulnerable to their charms, especially if they offer solutions and services the person believes they need help with.

To prevent exploitation from strangers coming to the door, ask your parent what help they need around the home. With their agreement, make appointments with creditable services on their behalf. Ask neighbours for recommendations of local businesses and services when needed. Also ask that neighbours alert you to the appearance of dodgy door-to-door salespeople who target the neighbourhood – and then advise your parent of their existence so they have time to prepare a response, should they be targeted.

# Legal and Financial Matters

- Talking finances and preparing for future care costs
- Power of Attorney
- Dubious Family Characters
- Appointing Guardians and Financial Managers
- Aged Care Facilities
- Wills
- Advanced Care Directives/Living Wills
- Euthanasia

## TALKING FINANCES AND PREPARING FOR FUTURE CARE COSTS

Our parents grew up in a time when speaking about money was considered crass. Hence initiating conversations with them about how they will fund their later years can take some careful consideration. This essential conversation should be conducted well before the emergence of a health crisis or suspected cognitive deterioration.

Not having an agreed-to plan of action – should the need arise – may result in your parent being forced into a situation that they would never have chosen for themselves. It may also mean that you and your siblings are left with some hefty bills to pay.

*Essential items to include in a conversation on finances:*

- Source of income. Does your parent receive a government pension, superannuation payments, income from private investments – or a combination of payments?
- Do they own their own home?
- Do they have other properties or investments that may impact on access to facilities and services that have a means-tested payment plan.

- Do they have a current comprehensive health insurance policy? Will this insurance plan cover private hospitals, specialists in private practice, and community based health services? Are they reliant on government funded health care services (with longer waiting lists than private services)?
- If your parent needs financial help to pay for health care – where will this money come from?

Getting old can be expensive. It can be a time that requires some financial savvy. Most importantly it is a time that default plans are often summoned to ensure that the older person is financially able to access the health and community care they require but are unable to arrange for themselves.

The emergence of financial advisors specializing in post-retirement clients continues to grow – and paying for this service is definitely worth the expense for people with wealth, complicated finances, and dysfunctional families.

*What Can You Do to Help Ensure Your Parent Has Adequate Finances to Cover Their Later Years?*

Ideally your parent has plans in place that cover various possible later life scenarios. In this case your job (should your parent need assistance) will be to:

- Research the current cost and availability of services and facilities;
- Evaluate whether your parent continues to have adequate finances to cover whatever care they need; and,
- Come up with more affordable options, or additional money, should this be required.

If your parent has not made arrangements, you might provide support by accompanying them to appointments with financial advisors, lawyers and relevant government offices (related to pensions, etc) – during a visit. If not, be available to talk openly with them about these appointments, as they can be a source of stress.

We would all like to believe that our parents, our partners and ourselves, are not going to succumb to a dementing illness. Yet by the age of 80, one in four people do have a dementia, so ignoring this possibility is unrealistic. Making plans to cover this health problem (if it does occur) is smart and will save considerable frustration and problems in years to come.

## Power of Attorney

Let's say I was hit by a bus and ended up in a coma for three weeks. How would my family access the funds in my bank account to pay any important outstanding bills I accrue during my hospitalization? If my parent suffered a stroke and was unable to return home after a lengthy hospital stay – how could I sell the family home to pay for admission to a long stay facility?

The solution and ease by which both scenarios can be managed is going to depend on whether the person (me or my parent respectively) has appointed a Power of Attorney. Without a Power of Attorney – it will be almost impossible to assist in matters that demand access to the person's finances.

In general, appointing a Power of Attorney is an easy process that involves downloading and completing the appropriate documentation. These documents are then witnessed and lodged with the relevant legal authority. As a social worker I strongly recommend appointing an Enduring Power of Attorney – someone who has the legal capacity to act on your behalf should you become mentally incompetent.

## Dubious Family Characters

Unfortunately there are some family members who do not have their parents' best interests at heart. In my professional life I have encountered older people who have had their home sold or rented out by a family member - while they have spent extended periods lying in a hospital bed unaware of the completed real estate deal. Obviously this exploitation of elderly parents can leave irreparable rifts in families. It can also result in a lack of available options for the older person when it is time to be discharged from the hospital. These cases often require legal interventions and the appointment of a guardian and/or financial manager.

## Appointing Guardians and Financial Managers

Twenty years ago, I worked at the NSW Guardianship Board (now a division of NCAT) investigating applications to have guardians and financial managers appointed, and preparing the matters to be heard before the Board. The majority of applications were for older people with dementia who were in hospital and refusing discharge to an aged care facility.

This common scenario is often the reason that medical staff and hospital management refuse admission to elderly clients. Patients want to be discharged home, yet the safety risks of sending them home places medical staff in jeopardy of neglecting their 'duty of care' oath.

Discharging to a care facility may require the appointment of a guardian with powers of accommodation and health care. Frequently, an application to appoint a financial manager is also required because the person did not appoint an Enduring Power of Attorney before the onset of their dementia. Hence, arrangements to protect the person (both physically and financially) are made by the government.

Before appointing a guardian or financial manager the relevant legal board needs to ascertain:

- the person's ability to manage their own affairs
- the existence of relevant medical or health conditions that will impact on the person's ability to make decisions, like dementia, mental

illness, intellectual disability, or acquired brain injury, and
- that the appointment of a guardian and/or a financial manager is in the best interests of the person. (Australian Government 2015)

## Aged Care Facilities

Before your parent moves into an aged care facility, it is recommended that you read all the fine print on the contract. If you don't understand the contract seek legal advice.

*The questions to consider include:*

- Is there a bond required? If so, will the bond be returned if your parent moves or dies? Will the complete bond be returned or only a proportion?
- What are the fees? Is there a different fee for people receiving government pensions and people living off their own savings or superannuation?
- Do residents need to buy a place in the home? If so, when is the money required (some people will need to sell the family home to finance the move)? Again, what happens when the resident

moves or dies. Will their place be sold and the money returned to their estate or family?

- If your parents' needs increase, are there services available to help meet these needs? Do they entail extra costs? At what stage would the facility be unable to meet health care needs?
- What happens if your parent decides that they do not want to continue living at the facility after three months? Six months? Two years?
- What extracurricular activities are available? Social, sporting, hairdresser, dentist, church attendance, other?
- Does the facility have a policy to resolve conflict between residents and/or residents and staff members?
- In the case of health care emergencies – will the resident be taken to hospital, or need to wait for a doctor to come to the facility?
- Most importantly for people living away from their parents: Can you have a weekly appointment to speak to staff about how your parent – how he/she is coping; obvious concerns; and to ask questions? Is anyone available to help your parent make a phone call

to you? Is there a volunteer visitor program available?

## WILLS

Writing a legal Will, allows you to decide what will happen to your money, property and belongings after your death. Wills have been around since Ancient Greece (around 500BC) and are perhaps the easiest legal document to convince an older person to have.

There is no legal requirement that a Will needs to be drawn up by a lawyer – yet Wills made on scraps of paper at home can be open to interpretation inconsistent with the original plans. Again the law demands that the person is mentally competent at the time of writing the document.

## LIVING WILLS (A.K.A. ADVANCED CARE DIRECTIVES)

First proposed in 1969 by American lawyer, Louis Kutner, living wills aimed to help patients guide doctors about what treatments they would want, should the need arise, and should they become unable to communicate their wishes. In many countries, they have become a legal nightmare.

> They dealt with the problem that doctors often found it hard to accept that patients might prefer death to treatment, especially when the patients could not speak for themselves.
> (BBC 2014)

In practice an Advanced Care Directive should work like this: I complete the document and register it with the correct legal authority after discussing the form with my family. Ten years later I am in a serious car accident that leaves me in a vegetative state in hospital. According to instructions documented in my advanced care directive, I have indicated that should I ever be in a vegetative state with a less than 50% chance of recovery, no active treatment including artificial resuscitation should be given.

### *Will medical staff turn off the machines and let me die?*

There exists a multitude of complicating issues and philosophical arguments that will probably over-balance the decision to let me die. The first complication being: where is the actual living will? If it was written 10 years ago, does it still convey my current wishes? Who decides what 'recovery' means? If I am a 35-year-old with two small children, are doctors prepared to let me die? Would this be different is I was an 83-year-old widow? What if my spouse or parents oppose my documented wishes? What if I am in hospital in a state/province that doesn't recognize Advanced Care Directives (In Australia – Advanced Care Directives are state dependent and hence often invalid should you end up in a hospital located in another state)? What if hospital policy is to ignore the instructions written in Living Wills? And finally, who is going to be responsible for making the decision to turn off the machines?

While I can easily envisage the philosophical and legal quagmire this brings (Kollmorgen 2014), I strongly support the proposal of advanced care directives for everyone. My reason being that it forces awareness about our own vulnerability as humans including the inevitable fact that death is unavoidable.

Completing the document demands conscious decision-making about one's own life, and communication of our plans with the people close to us. At the very least, family members aware of the health care desires of one another - have the best chance of advocating should the need arise.

## EUTHANASIA

About two years ago my neighbour was euthanized in the dining room of her home. She had been fighting cancer for about 18 months and was obviously losing the battle. One day her daughter summoned me to their home, indicating that her mother would like to speak with me. My friend was lying in a bed placed next to the dining room table. I uttered the usual greetings and pleasantries learnt in my Dutch classes. Unfortunately, I hadn't learnt a worthy response to the statement: I just wanted to tell you that I am going to die on Thursday. I wanted to say goodbye.

By this stage in her disease I knew that she was dying. The shock came from the fact that she had taken control of the situation and had the plans in place to end her suffering in a manner that she could deal with. It was a plan that she had made over the previous six months with her family, her doctors and her lawyer.

Yes, I live in the Netherlands where more than 5306 people were euthanized in 2014. Even in the

Netherlands the topic continues to generate heated discussions about morality and mortality. (DutchNews.nl Oct 27, 2015)

Euthanasia offers terminally ill people the power to decide when they are ready to stop suffering, say goodbye to family and friends, and end their lives. It is legal in very few countries around the world. The laws are strict and the chemistry well researched. People with dementia or other cognitive impairment are ineligible for euthanasia.

If euthanasia is an option in the state your parent lives, please listen and keep an open mind should he or she want to discuss this topic with you. This is especially relevant if they have been diagnosed with a terminal disease, like cancer. Helping a parent to prepare and make the necessary arrangements is an unimaginable task – but so too is watching someone you are close to suffering from constant pain and discomfort as they wait to die. Most important: seek support for yourself during this period.

# Overview of Care For An Aging Parent

- Care basics
- Providing care from a distance
- Advanced care
- The final visit

As I come to the end of this guide, I am overwhelmed by images of older people I have been fortunate to meet throughout my life. Without exception, every person has had a unique situation. Combining personality, family, finances, culture, life history and health problems means that no two people (at any age) are going to present with the same problems. As such, they should all be treated as individuals - and not as another old lady with Alzheimer's Disease, or the old diabetic guy with leg ulcers, or as the person in bed 46. These people are our parents, family members and our future selves.

## Care Basics

*The essentials of providing care are as follows:*

- Early, open discussions with your parents about what they want to happen, should they need help in the future. This can often lead to your parents conducting their own research into services and facilities that they may require in their later years. Ideally discussions should include how they might pay for these services.
- Research: find out what is available in the local area and whether these services have waiting lists (especially if considering aged care facilities).
- Practical provisions in place: appointing an Enduring Power of Attorney, writing an Advanced Care Directive, a Will, and instructing a financial advisor – are all important tasks that demand that your parent is mentally competent.

- Adapting to Age: making things simpler in the home to reduce risks and increase independence over the long term.
- Ensure regular, clear lines of communication between you and your parent. Feeling confident in discussing difficulties is the first step in asking for help.
- Support in place – know where it can come from.

## Providing Care from a distance

*In addition to the points above, the following points are important when you live in a different town, city, or country from your parent:*

- Have the discussion at a time when you are together; as a Skype or regular phone call; or in extended written conversation in emails or letters.
- Do the research on the Internet – or when you are visiting.
- Hassle your parents to make the legal arrangements that will protect them when they need to be protected. If needed, when you visit, go with them to a lawyer to ensure they are prepared.

- During a visit, assess the house for risks. Often the task of throwing away things, or exchanging appliances is something that older people put off. Offer your suggestions to make life easier and safer to your parent/s – and help make the changes happen.
- Be in charge of maintaining open lines of communication. Don't be disappointed if more communication is coming from your side. Keep it easy – a postcard, a weekly phone call – but make it a regular occurrence.
- If you can't be there in person to visit your parent, look at all possibilities to have someone else visit each week. A family member, a friend, neighbour, old work acquaintance, community health worker, or volunteer – someone to say hello to and who will notice if there is a problem developing.

## Additional Points

*A few final suggestions:*

- Be creative. You know your parent. What is it that would brighten their day if they were spending the majority of their time inside the house due to illness and reduced mobility? Ideas include: a subscription to their favourite magazine or newspaper; photos of grandchildren; an audio book; a home visit from a hairdresser? With technology the opportunities to support our aging parents during times of poor health are numerous.

- Be prepared to change plans. Aging and illness is not necessarily a smooth road. If prior research has been done, then moving to a new plan suitable for increased or altered care needs – should not be traumatic. As a rule of thumb, when services are initially employed ensure that the level of help can be increased if the need arises, or, that the care of your parent will be transferred to a service that can offer more help.
- Caring for an aging parent can be stressful. This is especially so, if you have always had a close relationship with your parent and now live too far away from them to spend physical time together. Your own anxiety about how your parent is managing will impact on your personal life. Make sure that you have someone that you can talk with about your concerns, and do things to reduce your own stress.

## Final Visit

One day the inevitable will happen. For many adult children, there will be a warning that their parent is close to dying and a chance to hurry to their bedside to say goodbye. For others, it will be the phone call notifying you that your parent has died – and the trip back will be for a funeral.

The process now is not caring for your parent. It is about looking after yourself as you grieve.

> The reality is you will grieve forever. You will never 'get over' the loss of a loved one; you will learn to live with it. You will heal and you will rebuild yourself around the loss you have suffered. You will be whole again but you will never be the same again. Nor should you be the same nor should you want to be.
> (Kübler-Ross, Kessler 2005, p203)

# Closing Thoughts

Getting older is inevitable. In making plans with and for your aging parents, don't ignore the sobering fact that with every new day, you are also growing older. Well, I am. I must be - if my parents are slowing down, my husband sprouting white hair, and my children are facing the end of their school years. Hence the number one message in this book is: teach children to value family. If you don't have your own children, be present in the lives of children around you (nieces, nephews, the children of close friends). Teach them to be generous with their love and time. Strengthen and maintain the connections you have with them. In a world where responsibility and respect for older people are diminishing, family and friends become the default safety net.

The second message is - make your own plans. Think about what you want to happen when you are older. This should encompass more than what you plan to do when you retire. Your plans need to extend to a time when you are no longer independent and fully mobile. Make your plans concrete by appointing a Power of Attorney, completing an Advanced Care Directive, and writing a Will. Plan to downsize the family home to make life easier in your later years. Spread your wings and develop many, long-lasting social contacts.

This guide is written to help you provide care for your parents when you live away from them – and when they need help. It is also a reminder that aging is a life phase that hopefully we are all fortunate to achieve. Aging well is about planning; staying connected; knowing your resources; adapting your life to your abilities; and getting help when needed. Enjoy the ride.

"Old Age ain't no place for sissies"
Bette Davis

# ACKNOWLEDGEMENTS

The people and places in this book are all non-fictional. They all exist, although some of the wonderful people exist now only in memory format. The pleasure of knowing them, even for a brief time, has been all mine.

My husband, Maurice McGinley, has been instrumental in getting this book into a printable and presentable shape. Infuriating at times, I appreciate you and your help always.

Thanks to Catherine McGinley, for being my role model in growing older – interesting, connected, an intrepid, strong woman and a lover of good laughs.

My deepest gratitude for their editing prowess goes to Helen Latemore and Shelley O'Rourke. I would also like to thank Robin Pascoe and Tracy Brown for their encouragement to write.

Finally, I owe thanks to my own parents and family for all their support.

---

Ana McGinley

# Bibliography

"The great secret that all people share": Doris Lessing. Available from: www.brainyquote.com/search_results.html#jQiVCU6lgp7xmgOE.99. (Accessed 8 February 2015).

Penn State 2015, "Communication key when dealing with aging parents". Available from: www.sciencedaily.com/releases/2015/01/150128113828.htm. (Accessed 6 June 2015).

"Old age is not a disease": Maggie Kuhn. Available from: www.values.com/inspirational-quotes/3706-Old-Age-Is-Not-A-Disease- . (Accessed 1 March 2015).

Queensland Government Department of Health 2015, "Career Structure". Available from: www.health.qld.gov.au/employment/work-for-us/clinical/medical/career-structure/default.asp. (Accessed 20 April 2015).

"There's nothing that makes you more insane": Jim Butcher. Available from: www.azquotes.com/quote/407210. (Accessed 3 February 2015).

Drakakis, H 2013, "Carer-friendly policies need to reduce pressure on the 'sandwich generation'". The Guardian (online). Available from: www.theguardian.com. (Accessed 5 May 2015).

Holzhausen, E 2014, "Sandwich generation concern is growing". Available from: www.carersuk.org. (Accessed 5 May 2015).

Wikipedia 2015, "Book of Common Prayer" [online] Available at: https://en.wikipedia.org/wiki/Book_of_Common_Prayer#Literary_influence (Accessed 16 Oct. 2015).

Office of National Statistics 2013, "What are the top causes of death by age and gender?" Available from:

www.ons.gov.uk/ons/rel/vsob1/mortality-statistics--deaths-registered-in-england-and-wales--series-dr-/2012/sty-causes-of-death.html. (Accessed 16 May 2015).

Alzheimer's Association 2015, "What is Dementia?" Available from: www.alz.org/what-is-dementia.asp. (Accessed 3 March 2015).

Alzheimers.Net 2015, "2015 Alzheimer's Statistics" Available from: www.alzheimers.net/resources/alzheimers-statistics/. (Accessed 4 March 2015).

National Heart, Blood & Lung Institute 2015, "What is Coronary Heart Disease?" Available from: www.nhlbi.nih.gov/health/health-topics/topics/cad. (Accessed 1 September 2015).

Medicine Net 2015, "Heart Disease" Available from: www.medicinenet.com/heart_disease_coronary_artery_disease/article.htm. (Accessed 1 September 2015).

Maier, R 2014, *Heart Disease Statistics*. Available from: www.healthline.com/health/heart-disease/statistics#1. (Accessed 1 September 2015).

CDC - Centers for Disease Control & Prevention 2015, "Stroke". Available from: www.cdc.gov/stroke/index.htm. (Accessed 3 September 2015).

Stroke Foundation 2015, "Facts and Figures About Strokes". Available from: www.strokefoundation.com.au/. (Accessed 3 September 2015).

Science Daily 2014, "Cancer Statistics 2014: Death Rates Continue to Drop". Available from: www.sciencedaily.com/releases/2014/01/140107102634.htm. (Accessed 20 August 2015).

Cancer Research UK n.d., "Causes of Cancer and Reducing Your Risk". Available from: www.cancerresearchuk.org/. (Accessed 28 August 2015).

Wikipedia 2015, "Arthritis" [online] Available at: https://en.wikipedia.org/wiki/Arthritis . (Accessed 16 Oct. 2015).

Arthritis Care 2015, "What is Arthritis?" Available from: www.arthritiscare.org.uk/. (Accessed 20 November 2015).

"Hindsight is a wonderful thing": William Blake. Available from: www.azquotes.com/quote/864486. (Accessed 6 July 2015).

CDC – Centers for Disease Control and Prevention 2015, "Important Facts About Falls". Available from: www.cdc.gov/homeandrecreationalsafety/falls/adultfalls.html. (Accessed 1 September 2015).

Rao, SC, & Jorge, TG 2010, "Update on the Management of Constipation in the Elderly: New Treatment Options", Clinical Interventions in Aging, no.2, pp 163-171. Available from: www.ncbi.nlm.nih.gov/pmc/articles/PMC2920196/. (15 September 2015).

Miller, J 1993, "Alcohol Abuse Among the Elderly: A Growing, Often Hidden Problem", The New York Times 28 November 1993. Available from: www.nytimes.com/. (Accessed 5 June 2015).

Hitchcock, K 2015, "Dear Life", Quarterly Essay vol.57, pp7-154. Available from: www.quarterlyessay.com/essay/2015/03/dear-life/extract. (Accessed 21 October 2015).

ABC News 2014, "Elderly Men Three Times More Likely to Die by Suicide", 27 March 2014. Available from: www.abc.net.au/news/2014-03-27/elderly-men-three-times-more-likely-to-die-by-suicide/5349116. (Accessed 6 May 2015).

"I love driving behind old people": author unknown. Available from: www.kappit.com/search/i-love-driving-behind-old-people/. (Accessed 27 Feb 2015).

Folstein, MF & Folstein SE 2010, "Mini Mental State Examination" 2ed., Florida: Psychological Assessment Resources.

CARRS-Q Centre for Accident Research and Road Safety Queensland 2015, State of the Road. Available from:
www.carrsq.qut.edu.au/publications/corporate/older_roaduser_fs.pdf. (Accessed 3 March 2015).

Australian Government Department of Social Services 2015, "Guardianship and Administrators". Available from: http://www.myagedcare.gov.au/financial-and-legal/guardianship-and-administrators. (Accessed 4 June 2015).

BBC 2014 "Ethics Guide – Living Wills". Available from: www.bbc.co.uk/ethics/euthanasia/overview/livingwill s.shtml. (Accessed 4 August 2015).

Kollmorgen, A 2014, "Want Control Over Your Final Days?" Available from: www.choice.com.au/health-and-body/healthy-ageing/ageing-and-retirement/articles/advance-care-directives. (Accessed 4 August 2015).

DutchNews.nl 2014 "Euthanasia Death Total Rises10% in 2014". Available from: www.dutchnews.nl/news/archives/2015/10/euthanas ia-death-total-rises-10-in-2014/. (Accessed 7 October 2015).

Kübler-Ross E & Kessler D 2005, "On Grief and Grieving: Finding the Meaning of Grief Through the Five Stages of Loss". New York: Scribner.

"Old Age Ain't No Place for Sissies" Bette Davis. Available from: www.brainyquote.com/quotes/quotes/b/bettedavis12 6805.html. (Accessed 7 November 2015).

Made in the USA
Charleston, SC
01 March 2016